Night, Leporello, Don Giovanni, Figaro, Susanna—here they all are, where light and shadow meet. Mozart opera in shadowgraph. The finely detailed silhouettes do more than sketch the outline of the plots—they conjure up the music itself.

On the following pages, in the order of their appearance on stage, are some dramatic moments from *The Marriage of Figaro, Don Giovanni, Così Fan Tutte,* and *The Magic Flute.*

LA VENDETTA, OH LA VENDETTA!
(REVENGE, YES, REVENGE!)

NON SO PIU COSA SON, COSA FACCIO...
(I NO LONGER KNOW WHAT I AM, WHAT I'M DOING...)

SUSANNA, IL CIEL VI SALVI...
(SUSANNA, HEAVEN BE WITH YOU...)

FERMATEVI...
(NO, STOP...)

SENTITE...
(LISTEN...)

SORTIRE ELLA NON PUO.
(SHE CAN'T COME OUT.)

CHE SOAVE ZEFFIRETTO QUESTA SERA SPIRERA...
(HOW SWEET THE BREEZE WILL BE THIS EVENING...)

SUSANNA, TU MI SEMBRI AGITATA E CONFUSA.
(SUSANNA, YOU SEEM TO BE AGITATED AND CONFUSED.)

VOI CHE SAPETE CHE COSA E AMOR...
(YOU LADIES, YOU KNOW WHAT LOVE IS...)

VENITE, INGINOCCHIATEVI...RESTATE FERMO LI.
(COME, KNEEL DOWN...STAY STILL HERE.)

VEDRO MENTRIO IO SOSPIRO, FELICE UN SERVO MIO?
(MUST I SEE A SERF OF MINE MADE HAPPY, WHILE I AM LEFT TO SIGH?)

IL BIGLIETTO...
(THE TICKET...)

ECCOMI A' VOSTRI PIEDI...
(HERE I KNEEL AT YOUR FEET...)

AH...SOCCORSO!...
(AH! HELP!...)

SON TRADITO!...
(I AM UNDONE!...)

LA CI DAREM LA MANO, LA MI DIRAI DI "SI."
(THERE WE'LL TAKE HANDS, AND YOU WILL SAY "YES.")

DEH VIENI ALLA FINESTRA, O MIO TESORO...
(O COME TO YOUR WINDOW, MY TREASURE...)

NON MI DIR, BELL'IDOL MIO, CHE SON IO CRUDEL CON TE...
(SAY NOT, MY BELOVED, THAT I AM CRUEL TO YOU...)

AH CHI MI DICE MAI QUEL BARBARO DOV'E?
(OH, WHO CAN TELL ME NOW WHERE IS THE KNAVE?)

MADAMINA, IL CATALOGO E QUESTO...
(LITTLE LADY, THIS IS THE LIST...)

BATTI, BATTI, O BEL MASETTO, LA TUA POVERA ZERLINA...
(BEAT ME, DEAR MASETTO, BEAT YOUR POOR ZERLINA...)

MI TRADI QUELL'ALMA INGRATA...
(THAT UNGRATEFUL MAN BETRAYED ME...)

PENTITI, CANGIA VITA: E L'ULTIMO MOMENTO!
(REPENT, CHANGE YOUR WAY OF LIFE: YOUR HOUR OF DOOM IS NEAR!)

AH GUARDA, SORELLA, SE BOCCA PIU BELLA...
(AH, TELL ME SISTER, IF ONE COULD EVER FIND A SWEETER MOUTH...)

DI PASTA SIMILE SON TUTTI QUANTI...
(ALL OF THEM ARE MADE OF THE SAME STUFF...)

AH, CHE TUTTO IN UN MOMENTO SI CANGIO LA SORTE MIA!
(AH, HOW MY LOT HAS CHANGED ALL IN A MOMENT!)

UN CONTRATTO NUZIALE!
(A MARRIAGE CONTRACT!)

AH SIGNOR, SON REA DI MORTE...
(AH, MY LOVE, MY SIN IS MORTAL...)

SMANIE IMPLACABILI CHE M'AGITATE…
(IMPLACABLE PANGS, WHICH TORMENT ME…)

ALLA BELLA DESPINETTA VI PRESENTO, AMICI MIEI…
(I PRESENT YOU, MY FRIENDS, TO PRETTY MISS DESPINA…)

E NEL TUO, NEL MIO BICCHIERO SI SOMMERGA…
(IN YOUR GLASS AND MINE…)

TE LO CREDO, GIOIA BELLA, MA LA PROVA FAR NON VO'.
(I BELIEVE YOU, MY FAIR ONE, BUT I WON'T PUT IT TO THE TEST.)

ZU HILFE! ZU HILFE!...
(HELP! HELP!...)

SONST BIN ICH VERLOREN...
(FOR I AM LOST...)

HE SKLAVEN! LEGT IHR FESSELN AN!
(HERE, SLAVES! CHAIN HER UP!)

ALLES FÜHLT DER LIEBE FREUDEN...
(EVERYONE FEELS THE JOY OF LOVE...)

ACH, ICH FÜHL'S, ES IST VERSCHWUNDEN!
(AH, I SENSE IT HAS VANISHED!)

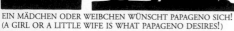

EIN MÄDCHEN ODER WEIBCHEN WÜNSCHT PAPAGENO SICH!
(A GIRL OR A LITTLE WIFE IS WHAT PAPAGENO DESIRES!)

ICH KANN NICHTS TUN, ALS DICH BEKLAGEN...
(I CAN DO NOTHING EXCEPT PITY YOU...)

ER IST'S. SIE IST'S! ICH GLAUB ES KAUM!
(IT IS HE! IT IS SHE! I CAN'T BELIEVE IT!)

EWIG HIN DER LIEBE GLÜCK!
(THE JOY OF LOVE GONE FOREVER!)

PA-PA-PA-PA-PAPAGENO! PA-PA-PA-PA-PAPAGENA!
(PA-PA-PA-PA-PAPAGENO! PA-PA-PA-PA-PAPAGENA!)

CONTENTS

MOZART
FROM CHILD PRODIGY TO TRAGIC HERO

Michel Parouty

DISCOVERIES
HARRY N. ABRAMS, INC., PUBLISHERS

On 27 January 1756 a powdery snow was steadily falling on the town of Salzburg, in Bavaria. In No. 9 Getreidegasse, Leopold Mozart was pacing up and down like a caged animal. From the next room he could hear muffled sounds of footsteps and whispering: His beloved wife, Anna Maria, was about to give birth to their seventh child. It was a boy. They called him Wolfgang.

CHAPTER I

A CHILD PRODIGY AT THE COURTS OF EUROPE

The Mozart family occupied one floor of a large house on the Getreidegasse, seen here (left) in an engraving from the 19th century, when it had already become a place of pilgrimage for music lovers. Right: Mozart sentimentalized in porcelain.

S alzburg in Mozart's
time (above): A
principality with about
10,000 inhabitants.

"Leopold [opposite] was
quite an average person,
devoid of genius. But
he possessed talent, and
his treatise on violin
playing and some of his
church sonatas amply
demonstrate the strong
pedagogical influences
that were to mark
Wolfgang's early studies.
Wolfgang's mother
[left], though lively,
even-tempered, and
imaginative, appears to
have been somewhat
passive and superficial,
and we get no clear
picture of her even from
the later references by
her children.**"**
    Mozart biographer
    Emmanuel Buenzod
    1930

Leopold Mozart was thirty-seven when Wolfgang was
born. He had grown up in a family of bookbinders in
Augsburg, Germany, but he had chosen a career in
music. At the age of twenty-four, he was a violinist in
the orchestra of the archbishop of Salzburg, Prince
Siegmund von Schrattenbach, later becoming court
composer and finally vice Kapellmeister (assistant
music director). He was a prolific writer of
compositions that were functional, well crafted, and
easy on the ear but not distinguished enough to bring
him fame, although a certain renown came his way
with the publication in 1756 (the year of Wolfgang's
birth) of his *Violin Method,* still a valued reference
work for violinists. For forty years, Leopold faithfully

carried out his duties to the archbishop, though he frequently lamented the ingratitude with which his efforts were rewarded.

In 1747 Leopold married Anna Maria Pertl, the daughter of a civil servant. Their marriage endured separations and sorrows—five of their children did not survive infancy. Wolfgang's only surviving sibling was Maria Anna (nicknamed Nannerl). She was four and a half when he was born.

Wolfgang and Nannerl's maternal grandfather had also been a musician, and it was natural that the two Mozart children should grow up immersed in music. Leopold, a knowledgeable and cultivated man, educated his children carefully. His lessons, while serious, were varied and stimulating; Wolfgang became fascinated by mathematics. Nannerl, at the age of eight, began to learn the harpsichord, and her brother listened.

Three-Year-Old Wolfgang Sat at the Harpsichord Searching Out Notes "That Like Each Other"

His progress was phenomenal. He began to compose before he could write. As early as 1761, when barely six, he showed his first compositions to his father,

Nannerl, at the age of eleven. Though herself a child prodigy, she was soon overshadowed by her younger brother.

who was quite overcome. The boy's precocious talent and desire to learn were beyond doubt. Much later, Johann Andreas Schachtner, a court trumpeter and violinist, recalled, "One day Wolfgang was busy scribbling away. His father asked what he was writing. 'A keyboard concerto; I've nearly finished the

The suit of clothes worn by the six-year-old Wolfgang in this portrait was given him by Empress Maria Theresa; it was a castoff from her son Maximilian.

first part.'" Leopold looked dubiously at the clumsy, childish manuscript and marveled: Wolfgang, already capable of intense concentration, was a musician through and through.

Naturally, the children's gifts had to be promoted, and clearly the best way to do this was to travel.

In 1762 the Family Left Salzburg Led by a Leopold Eager to "Show the World a Miracle"

Their first tour, to Munich, then the capital of Bavaria, is not documented. The second was to Vienna, seat of the Hapsburgs—the ruling family of Austria since the 13th century—and outlying towns.

Though Nannerl played the harpsichord brilliantly, it was her brother who stole the show, as countless anecdotes record. By the time the family arrived in Vienna on 6 October, everyone was already agog to see and hear the child prodigy. The Mozarts were immediately in demand at all the best houses. They had been there barely a week when Joseph II, eldest son of the Empress Maria Theresa and future Holy Roman emperor, insisted that his mother grant the family an audience at Schönbrunn, the royal summer palace. There the empress allowed the boy to jump into her lap, fling his arms around her neck, and give her a big kiss. The entire court was enraptured by the confident little boy for whom nothing seemed too difficult, even playing a keyboard hidden by a cloth.

At Schönbrunn, a little girl no older than Wolfgang helped him up when he slipped on the floor. "That was very kind of you," he said to her gratefully. "When I grow up I will marry you." The girl was Maria Theresa's daughter Marie Antoinette, future queen of France. It is not known how she responded to his proposal.

Leopold Mozart attentively watches as his son composes (opposite). In this scene imagined by a 19th-century artist, the visitor on the right is probably Schachtner, owner of a violin whose sweet full tone prompted the young Wolfgang to call it the "butter violin."

The violin Wolfgang played as a child (left).

On its journey to Vienna, the family was exempted from paying the local customs dues, thanks to little Wolfgang. "For he at once made friends with the customs officer, showed him the square piano, invited him to visit us and played him a minuet on his little violin, and we were allowed through" (Leopold Mozart, letter of 16 October 1762).

Vienna, City of Ceremonies

A gala performance at the Hofburg (the imperial palace) on the occasion of the marriage of Archduke Joseph, Maria Theresa's eldest son, and Isabella of Parma in 1760. The marriage of a prince was a good pretext for sumptuous festivities calculated to impress the populace. And what could be more alluring than the prospect of employment in the capital of the empire? In the figure of one of the boys in the front row (detail below), we can imagine we see the young Wolfgang, who would be welcomed at the Viennese court two years later.

Music Capital of Europe

Seat of the Holy Roman Empire from 1558 to 1806, Vienna was a prosperous city whose population during the reign of Maria Theresa rose from 88,000 to 175,000. The Austrian capital was a city known for welcoming all visitors, including foreigners. This tradition lasted until well into the 20th century, and the varied influences were reflected in all branches of art. As the center of the empire, Vienna played host to all of Europe, especially during the 1700s. Its exceptional vitality reached a climax at the end of the 18th century under the aegis of the imperial family and was especially manifested in brilliant musical and artistic displays.

Detail of a scene at the wedding feast of Joseph and Isabella.

The schedule of concerts and receptions was hectic, and at the end of the second week, an exhausted Wolfgang was confined to his bed. He quickly recovered, but the pace had to slacken. Soon it was time to leave. On 5 January 1763, after a rewarding detour to Pressburg (now Bratislava), in the former Czechoslovakia, the family returned home. They brought with them two sumptuous suits of clothes for Wolfgang, both gifts from Empress Maria Theresa, and the satisfaction of instant fame. But this was not to last. The excitement of the early days would wane, and Wolfgang found that the fickle Viennese public was quick to lose interest.

Even in the Age of Enlightenment, When Freedom and Humanitarianism Were the Purported Ideals, Musicians Were Still Only Servants

Soon after his return, Wolfgang became ill, and he used the period of rest to polish his violin playing. On 9 June the entire family set off again, this time on a great three-year odyssey.

Leopold's letters from this period give us vivid insight into the life of a musician in the 18th century. Reality had little in common with the romantic vision of the artist in an ivory tower, living for art alone. Unsalaried, instrumentalists, singers, and composers

Above left: The young Mozart being presented at the Viennese court. "We were there from 3 to 6 o'clock, and the Emperor himself... made me go and hear the Infanta play the violin" (Leopold Mozart, letter of 16 October 1762).

had to be resourceful and not rely too heavily on the generosity of the nobility. The presents Wolfgang did receive (watches, snuffboxes, and so on—he soon had a fine collection) could not guarantee the daily bread.

Europe in the mid-18th century. At this time, Germany was made up of small independent principalities.

From Court to Palace, the Mozart Family Traveled the Roads of Europe

On the way to Munich they were held up in Wasserburg by a broken carriage wheel, and, in an

impromptu recital, Wolfgang astonished the audience with his cleverness at playing a pedal organ without ever having been taught. Finally they reached Munich and the court of Maximilian III, elector of Bavaria, where they were well rewarded and given warm letters of recommendation.

Things did not always go so well. At Augsburg, for instance, where the children performed in front of a public audience for the first time, their reception was disappointing. And the duke of Württemberg refused even to hear them. Traveling northwest to Mannheim, they were more kindly treated by Elector Karl Theodor, for whom they played at Schwetzingen and in whose summer residence they were lucky enough to hear the Mannheim orchestra—considered the best ensemble of the day.

On they went, to Worms, Mainz, and Frankfurt, where the young Johann Wolfgang von Goethe (1749–1832) was in the audience. Later the poet would reminisce about the "little fellow with his wig and sword." Koblenz and Bonn followed, then Cologne and Aachen, where Princess Amelia, sister of Prussian King Frederick the Great, is reported to have smothered Wolfgang with caresses.

Several stops later they arrived in Brussels, which was then the capital of the Austrian Netherlands and governed by Charles of Lorraine, brother of Francis I, Empress Maria Theresa's husband. And finally, on 18 November 1763, the family arrived in Paris, where

Augsburg, Bavaria, in the 18th century, a center of commerce and banking. Below: A flute-maker from Augsburg.

Opposite above: Wolfgang and the Marquise de Pompadour.

Count Maximilian von Eyck, son-in-law of the grand chamberlain at the Salzburg court, made them welcome at the Bavarian embassy.

Below: Baron Friedrich Melchior von Grimm.

In the French Capital, the Mozarts Met a Ministering Angel: Baron von Grimm

German Baron Friedrich Melchior von Grimm (1723–1807), a passionate advocate of Italian music, had lived in France for thirty years. He moved in popular French literary circles and was known throughout Europe for his *Literary, Philosophical, and Critical Correspondence* (1753–90), a compilation of his letters to royalty in Germany, Russia, Sweden, and Poland, in which he discusses intellectual life in France. It was an article Grimm wrote on 11 December 1763 that provided the best possible introduction of the Mozarts to Parisian society. News of their arrival spread like wildfire, and the entire aristocracy, ever eager for novelty, became completely obsessed with them. At the end of December, they were received at the palace of Versailles, home of King Louis XV, and smothered in embraces by most of the ladies, though not—Wolfgang noted sadly—by the Marquise de Pompadour, the king's mistress. They were even invited to the traditional New Year's Day banquet.

More important than any socializing, however, were their encounters with other musicians.

Tea with a Prince

This genre painting was made by Michel Barthélemy Ollivier in the summer of 1766, during Wolfgang's second visit to Paris. It is set in the Mirror Room of the Palais du Temple, residence of the Prince de Conti. The ten-year-old boy is barely visible behind the harpsichord. Next to him stands the tenor Pierre Jélyotte. A favorite performer of Jean-Philippe Rameau's works, Jélyotte was also a violinist and guitarist in the king's orchestra and is seen here tuning his instrument. It is typical of 18th-century French society that members of the assembled company are paying little attention to the music but are carrying on with what they are doing, so that, as he complained years later (again in Paris), Wolfgang "had to play to the chairs, tables and walls" (letter of 1 May 1778).

In Paris, Wolfgang Met Johann Schobert, a German Composer

SONATES
POUR LE CLAVECIN
Qui peuvent se jouer avec l'Accompagnement de Violon
DEDIÉES
A MADAME VICTOIRE
DE FRANCE
Par J.G. Wolfgang Mozart de Salzbourg
Agé de Sept ans
ŒVRE PREMIERE
Prix
Gravées par Mme Vendôme C.-devant rue S.t Jacques
à present rue S.t Honoré Fils à vis le Palais Royal.
A PARIS,
aux adresses ordinaires
AVEC PRIVILEGE DU ROI.

In a letter written in early February 1764, Leopold asserted that in Paris, French and Italian music were in a perpetual state of war, and he observed that a national French taste in music was disappearing. He also lauded the contributions of the Germans, including harpsichordist Johann Gottfried Eckard of Augsburg, his colleague Johann Schobert, Hermann Friedrich Raupac, and others. Each had an influence on young Wolfgang, who four years later would take individual movements of sonatas written by these composers and rearrange them as harpsichord concertos.

Schobert (d. 1767) was a versatile musician, inventive and imaginative. His work, a blend of German, Italian, and French influences, could hardly fail to have an especial effect on so receptive a young mind. His influence is apparent in the works Mozart composed at that time, two pairs of sonatas for harpsichord with violin accompaniment (K. 6–7 and K. 8–9), which were published in Paris and dedicated respectively to Princess Victoire, daughter of King Louis XV, and the Comtesse de Tessé, lady-in-waiting to the king's daughter-in-law. ("K." stands for Baron Ludwig von Köchel, who in 1862 published a chronological catalogue of Mozart's compositions, assigning a number to each work for easier reference.)

The first important compositions by the seven-year-old boy are the two sonatas for harpsichord with violin accompaniment (K. 6–7) written during the winter of 1763–4 (title page, top). Above: A French harpsichord built in 1716.

A concert (detail from an 18th-century painting).

Toward the end of the 18th century, the harpsichord was displaced in popularity by the pianoforte (in its first, wood-framed form sometimes called a fortepiano). As a virtuoso performer, Wolfgang appreciated the instruments of his day, and in 1777 he was quick to enthuse over the products of the Augsburg piano manufacturer Johann Andreas Stein. Unlike the harpsichord, where the strings are plucked, the pianoforte (literally, "soft-loud") has an action in which the strings are struck by hammers, allowing greater gradations of dynamics from "pianissimo" (very soft) to "fortissimo" (very loud) and a wide variety of touch. Further modifications led to the development of the modern piano.

In London Wolfgang Discovered the Sunshine of Italy in the Music of Johann Christian Bach

On 10 April 1764 the family left Paris for Calais, a coastal town in northern France, where they boarded a boat to Dover, England. On 23 April they arrived in London, and four days later they were received by King George III and Queen Charlotte. The relaxed atmosphere at the English court was most welcome after the formality of Versailles. On 19 May Wolfgang and Nannerl gave a private concert to an appreciative royal family: Wolfgang improvised compositions, sight-read music by others, played the violin and organ, and accompanied the queen's singing.

In Paris the dominant musical influences had been German, but in London they were Italian. Paradoxically, this was due in part to a German, Johann Christian Bach (1735–82), youngest son of the great Johann Sebastian (1685–1750). He had worked as a composer and organist in Italy for several years. The younger Bach would become one of Wolfgang's closest friends.

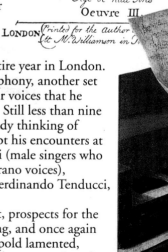

Six Sonates pour le Clavecin qui peuvent se jouer avec L'accompagnement de Violon ou Flaute Traversiere Très humblement dediées A SA MAJESTE CHARLOTTE REINE de la GRANDE BRETAGNE Composées par I.G. WOLFGANG MOZART Agé de huit Ans Oeuvre III. LONDON Printed for the Author at Mr Williamson in...

The Mozart family spent an entire year in London. Wolfgang composed his first symphony, another set of sonatas, and an anthem for four voices that he presented to the British Museum. Still less than nine years old, Wolfgang was also already thinking of composing an opera, and no doubt his encounters at this time with two famous castrati (male singers who are castrated to preserve their soprano voices), Giovanni Manzuoli and Giusto Ferdinando Tenducci, strengthened his determination.

In spite of another visit to court, prospects for the second autumn looked less exciting, and once again the Mozarts had to move on. Leopold lamented, "The very sight of the luggage we have to pack makes me perspire. We have been in England for a whole year. Why, we have practically made our home here!" The family embarked at Dover on 1 August 1765 and passed through Calais, Dunkirk, Lille, Ghent, and The Hague in the Netherlands.

The Return Journey Entailed Several Stops, as the Mozarts Were Fêted Everywhere

In the Netherlands, Wolfgang performed for the Prince of Orange and his sister, Princess Caroline. Nannerl soon fell gravely ill with intestinal typhoid fever. Wolfgang continued to compose and perform until he too succumbed. Once they had recovered, the children gave two recitals in Amsterdam and took part in the installation celebrations for Prince William V before paying another visit to Paris. There they stayed two months, during which Baron Grimm again acted as a wonderful press agent. Paris, Lyons, Geneva, Lausanne, Bern, Zurich—no longer did they need to ask for invitations!

One slight worry was that the Mozarts had been away from Salzburg much longer than they had planned; but the archbishop was wise enough to realize that the glory they acquired abroad would reflect well on Salzburg.

The family was home on 30 November 1766. During this first tour of the courts of Europe, Wolfgang had not only become something of a legend but had had musical experiences far beyond those of a mere child prodigy.

Johann Christian Bach (above), portrayed here by English painter Thomas Gainsborough, revealed to Wolfgang the beauties of a melodic style that was less austere than that of the Germans.

Left: Wolfgang at the piano, and the title page of a set of sonatas. "Now I have the heavy expense of having six sonatas of our Master Wolfgang engraved and printed, which (at her own request) are being dedicated to the Queen of Great Britain" (Leopold Mozart, letter of 27 November 1764).

Wolfgang Mozart was now eleven and famous, many remarkable events already behind him. He had grown out of being a child prodigy, and his next task would be to show the world that, far from being merely a precocious brat, he was an outstanding musician. He turned first to Italy, the land of opera.

CHAPTER II
FROM CHILD PRODIGY TO COMPOSER

In Italy, the young Mozart (opposite) was enthusiastically received by the owners of such grand homes as the Villa Albani in Rome (above).

Eleven can be an awkward age. But Mozart in 1767 was no ordinary child. He loved being made a fuss of, playing games, joking, but he also adored work. The few months spent in Salzburg before setting off again were devoted to studying, and under his father's guidance he buckled down right away. Mozart already wrote deftly in three-part harmony, amusing himself by giving names to each of the parts: *Signor d'Alto, Marchese Tenore, Duca Basso* (Sir Alto, Lord Tenor, His Grace the Bass). His working speed was amazing.

George Frideric Handel (1685–1759, above), originally from Germany, chose to settle in London in 1712. He wrote his famous *Messiah* there in 1742.

In London Mozart had seen a musical world much influenced by Italy. Now, in a burst of patriotism, he turned his attention to German composers—Carl Philipp Emanuel Bach, Johann Eberlin, Johann Adolf Hasse, and George Frideric Handel.

Commissions flooded in not only from the court but from the bourgeoisie, too. He was asked to write one act of an oratorio (a dramatic, religious choral composition), to be performed on 12 March 1767, called *Die Schuldigkeit des Ersten Gebots* (*The Obligation of the First Commandment*). For this he collaborated with Johann Michael ("Michael") Haydn (1737–1806) and the organist Anton Cajetan Adlgasser (1729–77), both much older than himself. This was followed by a Latin comedy, *Apollo and Hyacinthus*, written for a celebration at the Salzburg university. In both works the conventional forms are permeated with Mozart's own uniquely personal warmth of expression.

In this way the months passed quickly, and then, in September 1767, the whole family left Salzburg again, this time for Vienna.

The Stay in Vienna Was Disappointing

Empress Maria Theresa's daughter Maria Carolina was about to marry Ferdinand, king of Naples, and it looked as if an excited city might offer a wealth of attractive opportunities to musicians. Alas, fate intervened cruelly: An epidemic of smallpox carried off the young bride. Leopold's chief desire was to

get his family away from the city as fast as possible. Too late: Wolfgang had been infected and was struck with the disease at Olmütz, in Bohemia, and Nannerl also fell ill. Mercifully, both recovered, and in early January the Mozarts returned to Vienna, where they stayed for a year.

But it was not an easy time. Mozart and his sister were now twelve and seventeen and had lost the curiosity value they had had as children. And yet the budding composer could not hope to compete with the great names of the day, such as Franz Joseph ("Joseph") Haydn (1732–1809,

Left and above: Two composers who were famous in Mozart's lifetime—Carl Philipp Emanuel Bach (1714–88) and Johann Adolf Hasse (1699–1783). First known as a singer, Hasse became a composer of Italian opera serias. He said of the young Mozart, "One day this child will eclipse us all."

Below: A Viennese street scene of around 1800.

Michael Haydn's older brother and a prolific writer of symphonies and chamber music) and Christoph Willibald Gluck (1714–87, a revolutionary opera composer, today credited with unifying opera's three main elements—drama, emotion, and music). Mozart had his first taste of jealousy and rivalry.

To Attract Attention to His Son, Leopold Urged Him to Write an Opera

Mozart needed little encouragement to attempt an opera, something he had wanted to do since his exposure to Italian opera in London. In 1768 he wrote *La Finta Semplice* (*The Sly Maiden*) to a libretto by Marco Coltellini based on a comedy by Carlo Goldoni. Though it was deemed "an incomparable work," the opera was kept off the stage for a year by the young composer's envious detractors. (It was finally performed not in Vienna but in Salzburg, for the birthday of the archbishop.) This delay was a bitter disappointment for Mozart. Consolation came, however, from an unexpected quarter: A wealthy music lover, Dr. Franz Anton Mesmer (originator of the theory of animal magnetism), commissioned him to write a short opera for his private theater. *Bastien and Bastienne* was premiered at Mesmer's home on 1 October 1768, in a friendly, intimate atmosphere that perfectly complemented its tale of rustic love affairs.

Enthusiastic as Ever, Wolfgang Devoured Italian Operas and German Symphonies

The final weeks of the stay in Vienna included another source of satisfaction for Mozart: the success of his first

Opposite: This portrait of an unknown musician suggests Mozart around the age of twelve.

"As for Wolfgang's opera [*La Finta Semplice*] all I can tell you is that...a whole hell of musicians has risen up to prevent the display of a child's ability.... A conspiracy has been formed to produce it...extremely badly and thus ruin it."
Leopold Mozart
14 September 1768

Christoph Willibald Gluck (below) was at the height of his fame in 1768, after composing the operas *Orfeo and Euridice* (1762) and *Alceste* (1767).

mass, the *Waisenhausmesse* ("Orphanage Mass," K. 139), written for the consecration of the new chapel of a court-sponsored orphanage. Leopold's letters tell proudly of the mass's success, "which has restored that reputation which our enemies, by preventing the performance of the opera, intended to destroy" (letter of 14 December 1768).

All in all, the material benefits of the journey were small, but they were offset by the musical ones. In those few months, Mozart was able to hear several popular Italian operas, including Hasse's *Partenope*, Nicola Piccinni's *La Buona Figliuola,* and Gluck's *Alceste* (which was to remain one of his favorites), and to absorb the new trends—led by Joseph Haydn, among others—that were revolutionizing the German symphonic scene. These two contrasting but complementary traditions combined to form the aesthetic framework of Mozart's entire subsequent career.

Meanwhile, in Salzburg, the archbishop had grown impatient with his itinerant employee and suspended Leopold's salary. Nevertheless, he welcomed them home warmly, putting the younger Mozart in charge of his court orchestra and soon granting father and son another leave of absence.

Siegmund von Schrattenbach, archbishop of Salzburg from 1753 to 1771. In Salzburg the archbishop held an aristocratic rather than an ecclesiastical position.

On 11 December 1769 Father and Son Set Off for Italy Alone

Nannerl, now eighteen, had become a fine piano teacher, and her lessons were bringing the household a substantial income; so while her brother and father visited Italy, she and her mother stayed at home.

Mozart had a happy temperament, and his letters home from this journey are full of gaiety—enthusiastic, droll, and still very childish, oddly lacking the sophistication so characteristic of his music. "Dearest Mamma! My heart is full of delight and pleasure, because I am so enjoying this journey; it is warm in the carriage and our coachman is a capital fellow who drives fast whenever the road gives him the slightest chance" (12 December 1769). Mozart was not yet fourteen, and he had every reason to feel happy. The first ports of call, Rovereto and Verona, in northern Italy, were made delightful by the exuberance of the Italians' welcome.

So thrilled was Mozart by Italy that he translated his middle name, Theophilus (Greek for "beloved of God"), into Italian. He had previously used the German form "Gottlieb"; now he signed himself "Amadeo" or "Amadé," which would eventually become the familiar Latin "Amadeus."

Success After Success in the Towns of Italy

In Mantua the audience at the Accademia Filarmonica gave an enthusiastic reception to a recital that consisted of fourteen pieces without a break. Mozart sight-read, played the

"Our city cannot but proclaim the remarkable musical abilities of the German boy Wolfgang Amadeus Mozart.… Last Friday, in a room in the illustrious Accademia Filarmonica and before a large assembly of the nobility of both sexes, this child gave such a display of his skills as to cause utter astonishment."
Gazzetta di Verona
9 January 1770

harpsichord and violin, sang, improvised, and performed some of his own compositions.

On 23 January 1770 the pair headed for Milan, where once again they were taken under the wing of a native of Salzburg, Count Karl von Firmian, governor of Lombardy and nephew of the previous archbishop. In Milan, the carnival season was coming to a climax, with concerts and operas galore. Piccinni was just putting the finishing touches on his opera *Cesare in Egitto* (*Caesar in Egypt*), which promised to be one of the highlights; Mozart and his father were invited to attend the dress rehearsal. They heard works by Luigi Boccherini (1743–1805), made the acquaintance of Giuseppe Sammartini (c. 1693–c. 1750), a composer who had been Gluck's teacher, and generally immersed themselves in Italian musical life.

One concert featuring Mozart was given on 23 February. Another was hosted by Count Firmian in the presence of "one hundred and fifty members of the leading nobility." Both were notable successes. Best of all, Mozart was commissioned to write an opera to be performed at the end of the year—an

Milan's Teatro Ducale (above), which opened in 1717, saw the first performances of Mozart's *Mithridates* and *Lucio Silla* and Hasse's *Ruggiero*. It burned down in 1776 and was replaced by La Scala, which opened two years later.

Padre Giovanni Battista Martini (1706–84, opposite), an Italian Franciscan monk, was famous throughout Europe as a composer, music scholar, and teacher.

opera seria (or tragic opera) this time, not an opera buffa (comic opera), as he had written in Vienna. In this genre, he would have to follow strict conventions of form: a somewhat tedious alternation of arias, to express emotion, and recitatives (partly sung, partly spoken narratives), to advance the action. Milan fell in love with Mozart.

Next stop was Parma, where Mozart was enchanted by the talents of Lucrezia Agujari, renowned for a remarkable singing voice with extraordinary range. Bologna followed, and here Mozart's one desire was to meet Padre Martini.

The enormous old Teatro Regio in Turin (above) has been replaced by one even larger.

Mozart's Knowledge of Italian Music Was Limited to the Fashionable Operas; Martini Introduced Him to the Old Masters

Padre Giovanni Battista Martini, then sixty-four years old, had been the teacher of Johann Christian Bach, Mozart's London friend. Besides being immensely talented as both a composer and a mathematician, he was the leading authority on all aspects of music theory. Closeted in the presbytery of San Francesco, from which he seldom emerged, he received Mozart twice and made him work through some arid exercises in counterpoint (the art of combining melodies). Mozart showed the venerable priest that, despite his youth, he was well versed in this skill.

This relationship would resume four months later, but meanwhile the Mozarts had an appointment in Florence, which was then a grand duchy governed by one of Maria Theresa's sons, Leopold. Here further successes awaited them, and here, too, they met up with old acquaintances from London, the violinist Pietro Nardini and the castrato Manzuoli. Mozart also uncharacteristically struck up a friendship with someone his own age, English violinist Thomas Linley (1756–78), from whom he parted with great reluctance.

The Mozarts arrived in Rome during Holy Week, and Leopold immediately took his son to various religious services, not so much out of piety but because this was the best way to meet useful people.

In Rome Mozart Displayed His Extraordinary Musical Memory

The famous *Miserere,* a choral work composed by Gregorio Allegri (1582–1652) in the early 16th century, was the exclusive property of the Sistine Chapel. Copying the manuscript was forbidden, although many had tried in vain to note it down while they listened. Mozart heard it twice and wrote the entire nine-part work out perfectly on a piece of paper he had hidden in his hat.

After a month in Rome, father and son moved on to Naples, where Mozart gave several concerts and enjoyed just being tourists and seeing the sights. A surprise awaited them on their return to Rome: Pope Clement XIV conferred on the fourteen-year-old Mozart the papal knighthood of the order of the Golden Spur, an honor that he shared with Gluck.

Part of the summer was spent in Bologna, Leopold nursing an injured leg while his son relaxed with the young Count Pallavicini and made several additional visits to Padre Martini, who gave him more and more themes for fugues and corrected his work with endless patience. It was thanks to this excellent mentor that on 9 October 1770, after a stiff examination, Mozart was admitted to the prestigious Accademia

St. Peter's Square, Rome.

"I only wish that my sister were in Rome, for this town would certainly please her, as St. Peter's Church and many other things in Rome are *regular*."
Mozart
14 April 1770

Pope Clement XIV (left) named Mozart a Knight of the Golden Spur in 1770.

Preceding pages: A painting by the 18th-century Roman artist Giovanni Paolo Pannini showing a musical entertainment in a fanciful setting.

Filarmonica of Bologna—an exceptional distinction, as he was below the usual requisite age of twenty.

While in Bologna, Mozart had acted the part of an assiduous pupil; back in Milan, he was already a universally acclaimed composer. Since the start of this journey he had composed only a few arias for his castrati friends and an early string quartet (K. 80), but now it was time to think about the opera that he had been commissioned to write. He began work in September, starting with the recitatives, deciding to leave the arias until he could judge the competence of the performers. "God be praised, the first performance of the opera [*Mitridate, Rè di Ponto*—

Mozart as a Knight of the Golden Spur. This portrait, painted in Salzburg in 1777, also mentions his membership in the musical academies of Bologna and Verona. Its formality is atypical: Mozart hardly ever wore the insignia.

CAV. AMADEO WOLFGANGO MOZART ACCAD. FILARMON: DI BOLOG. E DI VERONA

Mithridates, King of Pontus] took place on the 26th and won general applause.... Most unusually for a first night, an aria of the prima donna was encored" (Leopold Mozart, 29 December 1770).

Mozart returned to Salzburg in high spirits: Milan had requested another opera (*Lucio Silla*), Padua had commissioned an oratorio (*La Betulia Liberata*), and Maria Theresa had asked him to write a serenata (a secular cantata) to be played in Milan at the wedding of her son Ferdinand to Princess Maria Beatrice d'Este. Arriving home on 28 March 1771, Mozart had every reason to feel satisfied: The future looked full of promise, and he knew he would soon be back in his beloved Italy.

The days flew by. He wrote a few religious pieces and four symphonies, and soon it was time to leave again for Italy and four months of intense work.

In Milan the wedding festivities began on 15 October. On the 16th, Hasse's opera *Ruggiero* proved a failure, to everyone's surprise. Mozart's turn to face first-night nerves came the next day; but he need not have worried—his *Ascanio in Alba* was so well received that it was repeated two days later.

Mozart Discovered How Unpredictable People in Authority Can Be

Leopold had hoped to strike while the iron was hot: Why not attempt to obtain a permanent post for his boy in Milan? But he was unexpectedly turned away by Ferdinand. Could Maria Theresa have resented Mozart's success because the opera by Hasse, her own former Kapellmeister, had failed? Whatever the reason, her letter to her son (12 December 1771) is uncompromising: "You ask me to engage the young Salzburger in your service. I do not know why, not believing that you need a composer or useless people of that kind.... It lowers the tone when such people roam the world like beggars; and furthermore, he has a large family." Despite *Ascanio*'s success, Wolfgang had to leave Milan with no commissions at all.

A Cruel Disruption: On 16 December 1771 Archbishop Siegmund von Schrattenbach Died

Von Schrattenbach was succeeded by Count Hieronymus Colloredo. Intelligent and well-informed but stern and parsimonious, he was disliked and mistrusted by his subjects from the start. Proud of their independence, Salzburgers were worried about his relationship with the imperial family—he was a close adherent of Joseph II—and though Colloredo's administrative and cultural reforms may have been appropriate, they were far from popular.

Though he passed over Mozart's father in favor of Domenico Fischietti for the post of Kapellmeister, Colloredo appreciated Mozart's recent compositions (sacred works and church sonatas) and gave him the opportunity to write a theatrical entertainment for his installation festivities on 29 April. This was to be an opera, *Il Sogno di Scipione* (*The Dream of Scipio*), composed for a libretto by Pietro Metastasio (1698–1782), Vienna's court poet.

In October, Colloredo allowed his musicians to go to Milan for the premiere of *Lucio Silla*. Still, the Mozarts felt uneasy about the new archbishop, as is shown by their habit of writing in code when mentioning him in their letters.

A disturbing feeling of depression is reflected in the arias of *Lucio Silla*. Although Mozart had written six symphonies that summer, in the fall, for the first time, he had had trouble working.

The opera's December premiere was reported a success by Leopold, but even so, a feeler he put out to the grand duke of Tuscany about his son's possible employment had been completely ignored. On Mozart's return to Salzburg three months later, he had nothing more to hope for from Italy.

Opposite: The powerful and popular Maria Theresa, empress of Austria from 1740 to 1780, received Mozart kindly in 1762 but blocked his progress in 1771.

A cellist, by Jean Antoine Watteau. Stringed instruments of the 18th century sounded different from those of today. Steel strings are now more common than those made of animal gut, producing a tone that is clearer and stronger but less mellow.

Mozart's farewells to Milan were tinged with bitterness. He had recently been the darling of Italy, yet it had proved fickle and made no attempt to prevent his departure. He resigned himself to a life as court musician in Salzburg, but even a brief, exhilarating trip to Vienna could not dissipate the grayness of his native city.

CHAPTER III
MUSICIAN AND SERVANT

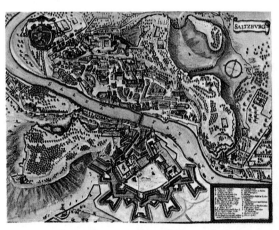

Mozart will always be associated with Salzburg, seen in the background of this 19th-century painting (opposite). Above: A map of Salzburg around 1600.

On 13 March 1773 Mozart and his father were back home in Salzburg. It is easy to imagine how depressed they were, since Leopold had not managed to secure for his son the permanent post in Italy he had hoped for—a post that would have been even better than the one he himself held at the court of the archbishop.

The Seventeen-Year-Old Ex-Prodigy Soon Began to Feel Suffocated in the Narrow Confines of His Native City

Mozart's last Italian journey had been undertaken without great optimism, yet he had composed continually. Besides completing *Lucio Silla,* he had written six more string quartets (K. 155–60). These show a strong Italian influence but are often infused with a deep melancholy. Some of the slow movements in particular, in poignant minor keys, betray his inner turmoil at this frustrating time.

Yet the same period saw the composition of *Exsultate, Jubilate* (K. 165), a vocal work that ends with a dazzling outburst of euphoria on the word "Alleluia." It remains one of the composer's most popular works today.

Mozart had always felt unfettered and free to travel, having spent his childhood and adolescence on the move. But now he found himself

Salzburg, dominated by a castle, stands beside the river Salzach. In the mid-18th century, it was an independent ecclesiastical principality: Even the Seven Years War, which broke out in 1756 and involved all the neighboring regions, did not disturb its tranquil routine. Nowadays Salzburg is in Austria, but it was incorporated only in 1816. Mozart, always loyal to his Bavarian origins, liked to think of himself as German. Opposite: Two views of the Salzburg castle.

Left: "My brother had been quite a good-looking child. But he was disfigured by smallpox, and, what is worse, he came back from Italy with a sallow complexion like an Italian's" (Nannerl Mozart). This gouache by Johann Nepomuk della Croce was probably painted in Salzburg in 1780.

enclosed in a town he hardly knew, trapped there by the obligations of his employment: Colloredo had confirmed his appointment at his court, which included playing first violin in the archbishop's orchestra. He was thus under an obligation to be both composer and performer.

Another man might have been happy with the security this provided, but not Mozart, who felt shackled by the staid, regular rhythm of Salzburg life, which utterly failed to give him musical satisfaction. Constantly in his mind was the example of his older colleague Michael Haydn, who was misunderstood by an audience that cared only for the tastes of the moment. It could hardly be expected that he, too, should bow to the demands of his profession if they were going to conflict with his desires and prevent him from writing the music he felt deep within.

A Position in Vienna Fleetingly Seemed a Godsend, but It Failed to Materialize

The ensuing weeks were devoted to fulfilling commissions from Italy for wind divertimenti (light, serenade-like compositions in several movements) and orchestral overtures. Meanwhile, Leopold had not given up trying to find his son a better post. Scarcely had he heard that the Kapellmeister at Vienna was seriously ill than they were packed and ready to leave.

It was, after all, very tempting. Here was a reasonable chance at a post as choir director of an opera house, a wonderful opportunity for a composer whose constant dream was of opera. In July therefore, during their weeks of leave, they traveled to the imperial capital. There they were granted an audience with Maria Theresa. "Her Majesty the Empress was indeed very gracious to us, but that was all" (Leopold Mozart, 12 August 1773). She left them with no illusions. Her attitude toward them had been clear enough in her letter to Ferdinand two years earlier.

The Congenial Atmosphere in Vienna Provided Mozart with a New Source of Inspiration

Despite financial difficulties, Mozart felt carefree in Vienna. He met up with his Viennese friends from earlier days, and although there was a lull in cultural activity during the summer months, he was alive to every whiff of the musical ferment that surrounded him and intoxicated his sensibilities.

It was the period of the German literary Sturm und Drang ("storm and stress") movement, characterized by opposition to tradition and an emphasis on individualism. The works of such writers as Gotthold Ephraim Lessing (1729–81) and Johann Wolfgang Goethe were finding their echoes in the music of Joseph Haydn and Gluck— high emotionalism driven by intense energy. It was no coincidence that Mozart's burst of symphonic activity in the spring was followed in the late summer by the sudden flowering of six string quartets (K. 168–73). Haydn's newest compositions—the famous set of

Opposite: Johann Wolfgang von Goethe, in a detail of a 1787 painting by Johann Heinrich Wilhelm Tischbein. Goethe once told a friend about seeing Mozart as a child in Frankfurt: "I saw him as a boy of seven, when he gave a concert when passing through. I myself was about fourteen, and I remember still quite clearly the little fellow with his wig and sword."

" I tell you before God, as an honest man: Your son is the greatest composer I know, either in person or by reputation; he has taste and, furthermore, he has the greatest mastery of the art of composition."
Joseph Haydn to Leopold Mozart, 1785

Left: Mozart and Haydn depicted in a wax bas-relief.

six string quartets (opus 20)—was also part of this welling-up of inspiration.

It was at this point that Mozart's aesthetic approach seems to have turned away from the jovial Italianate manner. An increased emotional seriousness is heard even in a serenade (K. 185) written in August in Vienna, perhaps to delight the guests at a wedding, perhaps for students at the University of Salzburg. But it becomes still more evident after the return to Salzburg in September.

The last months of 1773 were marked by renewed creative vigor. First there was a commission from Vienna for incidental music for a play, *Thamos, König in Aegypten* (*Thamos, King of Egypt*), concerned with the conflict between good and evil, light and dark.

Next came two symphonies, Nos. 25 (K. 183) and 28 (K. 200), in which Mozart's true voice is unmistakable. The former is written in his favorite tragic key of G minor and is deeply poignant. Symphony no. 28, now known to have been written before No. 25, is full of astonishing tension. This intense vein, amazing in a composer aged eighteen, continues in Symphony no. 29 (K. 201), written in 1774, which marks a decisive break with the earlier symphonies in the Italian tradition.

This Change of Direction in Mozart's Composition Was to Influence the History of an Entire Musical Genre

His originality and determination to turn his back on merely pretty entertainment were confirmed with even more brilliance in his first original piano concerto. (Four earlier ones had been little more than adaptations of pieces written by others.) The Piano Concerto no. 5 (K. 175) long remained one of his favorites: He revised it in Vienna in 1782, giving it a new finale. Its jaunty swing and jubilant character

Gala performance in Rome at the Teatro Argentina in 1747. The guests of honor are seated on the stage and surrounded by musicians on clouds. It was for just such occasions that Mozart's gifts were in demand.

are apt for a young man overflowing with vitality;
the inexhaustible melodic inventiveness, and the
treatment of the orchestra as partner rather than
accompaniment, reveal the accomplished master.

The vogue for the concerto grosso, in which a small
group of instruments is contrasted with a larger
group, had been at its height in the first half of the
18th century. The symphony, written for a large
orchestra, had later ousted it in popularity without,
however, impeding the development of another

form—the concerto for a single instrument and larger group. This became the soloist performer's preferred vehicle of expression. Mozart's imagination and theatrical sense found in the concerto an inexhaustible source of inspiration, enriched by influences from many quarters.

The Period of Exaltation Came to an End, and Mozart Returned to His Duties at Court

Religious pieces and works for special occasions formed part of his contractual obligations to the archbishop, and he wrote them without reluctance but without enthusiasm. Back in Salzburg, he was once more a servant, awaiting orders, supplying what was demanded. Such a situation could hardly be expected to satisfy so independent and creative a spirit.

Yet with his Symphony no. 30 (K. 202), dated 5 May 1774, he seemed to accept the situation and even to make concessions to the then-fashionable galant style—a form that contrasts with traditional counterpoint and is further illustrated in the Bassoon Concerto (K. 191), the Serenade no. 4 (K. 203), and also to some extent in the first six piano sonatas (K. 279–84). After all, that was what Colloredo and the Salzburg public demanded, and escape seemed impossible; even Joseph Haydn had to endure the same oppressive situation.

Leopold reacted in an unexpected way; years later, on 24 September 1778, he wrote, "It is better that whatever does you no honour, should not be made public. That is why I have not had any of your symphonies copied, because I know that when you are mature and have more insight, you will be glad that no one has got hold of them, even though at the time you composed them you were pleased enough with them."

Both Mozart's and Michael Haydn's names appear on this list of the musicians employed at the Salzburg court in 1775.

Opposite: Mozart at the spinet (an early harpsichord).

The Monotony of His Existence Was Broken by a New Commission, This Time from the Munich Court

Maximilian III, the elector of Bavaria, asked Mozart for a new opera buffa for the next carnival season in Munich.

Accompanied by his father, Mozart arrived in Munich at the beginning of December 1774, in bitter cold; Nannerl joined them soon afterward. They were received with great courtesy, and Mozart—with his work on the opera *La Finta Giardiniera* (sometimes known in English as *Sandrina's Secret*) already well advanced—felt perfectly at ease, despite suffering one of the painful gum abscesses to which he was prone. His letters from this period are full of good humor, abounding with puns and pseudo-Latin quotations.

The premiere of the opera had been scheduled originally for 29 December, but by the 20th, rehearsals had hardly begun. The performance was postponed until 13 January.

The Opera's Success Was Such That, Once Again, Everything Seemed Possible

The Mozarts began to hope for a commission for an opera seria, which was more prestigious for a composer than an opera buffa; all the more so because Mozart's success had eclipsed Antonio Tozzi's opera *Orfeo*, which had been billed as the climax of the carnival. "Thank God! My opera was performed yesterday, the 13th, for the first time and was such a success that I cannot describe the applause to Mamma.… Our return to Salzburg will not happen very soon, and Mamma should not wish it.… Mamma knows how good it is for me to be able to breathe freely. We shall come back soon enough" (Mozart, 14 January 1775).

Colloredo, however, passed through Munich during January and heard the praise being lavished on his employee without paying much attention. What he heard could not help but be less enthusiastic than what proud Leopold had reported to him. The more cautious critics were always careful to leave a note of

" I went to the theatre yesterday to see the comedy 'Mode nach der Haushaltung' ['The Fashionable Household'], which was very well acted.… Your Munich brother, the 1774th day of Anno 30, Dicembre. "
Mozart to his sister

Opposite: Inside the church at Au, a town near Munich.

" Wolfgang's opera went down so well at the first rehearsal that the performance has been postponed until 5 January to give the singers the chance to learn it better.… The composition of the music met with surprisingly great approval.… Now it all depends on the production in the theatre, and we hope that all will go well, for the actors are not ill-disposed towards us. "
Leopold Mozart
28 December 1774

Left: A view of Munich, showing the tower of St. Peter's church.

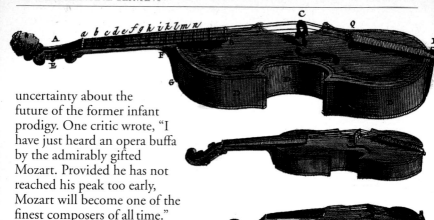

uncertainty about the future of the former infant prodigy. One critic wrote, "I have just heard an opera buffa by the admirably gifted Mozart. Provided he has not reached his peak too early, Mozart will become one of the finest composers of all time."

Mozart enjoyed the easy life of Munich, where he found it agreeable not to be treated like a servant for a change; to the contrary, he was even treated with deference.

It is thus hardly surprising that Mozart's stay was prolonged while *La Finta Giardiniera* received several more performances and two of his masses were heard in the court chapel. Perhaps to test the young man's professionalism as well as his talent, Maximilian III expressed a desire for a motet (a vocal work) in counterpoint. Mozart responded with the elaborate *Misericordias Domini* (K. 222).

But Mozart Left Munich Empty-Handed

Mozart was given no guarantee that he would be offered any position in Munich. His only commission was an unofficial one: A music-loving baron had requested some keyboard sonatas and bassoon pieces. Mozart took part in a friendly contest on the harpsichord such as were then fashionable, and then the family departed,

The violin is the ideal virtuoso instrument and the one with the greatest "singing" powers. Whenever Mozart wrote for the violin, he seemed to be thinking of the human voice and its incomparable expressive qualities.

Before 1775, Mozart had written only small violin concertos. Starting that year, he finally gave the instrument full-scale works to play.

arriving home on 7 March 1775. Mozart would have been surprised and disappointed if he had known that this time he would not leave again for thirty months.

A bove: *Still Life with the Violin*, an 18th-century painting by Jean Baptiste Oudry.

However, for a while all went well. The archbishop asked him to compose a theatrical entertainment for Maria Theresa's son Archduke Maximilian, visiting Salzburg on his way back to Vienna from seeing his sister Marie Antoinette at Versailles. This was the enchanting *Il Rè Pastore* (*The Shepherd King*). But once that excitement had died down, Mozart was

back to the old routine. His professional duties included playing the violin as well as composing, as Colloredo was quick to remind him. Nevertheless, between April and December 1775, he produced five violin concertos, of which two—No. 3 (K. 216) and No. 5 (K. 219)—show the composer triumphing over the limitations of the galant style and preserving his originality. The concertos testify to his talents as a violinist and also illustrate the various stages of the genre as it underwent rapid development at the time.

1776: Twenty-Year-Old Mozart Had No More to Hope for from Life in the Provinces

Mozart's existence in Salzburg seemed to be leading nowhere. Routine was tedious, and to make matters worse, Colloredo closed the court theater. Once more the story of Mozart's life can be traced in the list of works composed: masses, divertimenti, occasional pieces for local aristocrats. These included the *Serenata Notturna* (K. 239) for two small orchestras, the Piano Concerto no. 7 for three pianos (K. 242), and the Piano Concerto no. 8 (K. 246) written for a pupil—all works of supreme distinction, in which the hand of Mozart is unmistakable right from the first bars. But the most ambitious work of this period was the Serenade in D (K. 250), the *Haffner,* written for the wedding of Elisabeth Haffner, daughter of a prominent Salzburg businessman.

Archbishop Hieronymous Colloredo of Salzburg. The Mozarts referred to him as "the Mufti."

The latter part of the year was devoted to writing religious music, another requirement of his employment by the archbishop. He turned for counsel to Padre Martini, sending him the motet he had written in Munich and asking for his opinion. "Most reverend Padre Maestro, my esteemed Patron, the regard, the esteem and respect which I cherish for your illustrious person have prompted me to trouble you with this letter and to send you a humble specimen of my music, which I submit to your masterly judgment.... I live in a country where music has a struggle to exist.... The situation regarding the theatre is bad because of a lack of singers.... I amuse myself by writing chamber music and music for the church, in which branches of composition we have two other excellent masters of counterpoint, Signori Haydn and Adlgasser." The scholar's reply was courteous if a little formal, like an academic tutor's report. "I found the motet very pleasing...for it contains all the elements that modern music requires. ... I trust that you will continue to apply yourself unremittingly, for, by its very nature, music demands much study and practice throughout one's life."

Mozart Reached an Irrevocable Decision: He Would Leave Salzburg

Portion of a piano concerto in Mozart's hand.

Since the beginning of 1777, Mozart had produced just one significant work, the Piano Concerto no. 9 (K. 271). Its opening bars resound like an independence march, and it constitutes the first in a long series of piano concertos in which Mozart's genius flowered as nowhere else except, perhaps, in his operas.

Soon Leopold was contemplating another concert tour, with the ultimate aim of finding his son a better post. But Colloredo twice denied the request for a

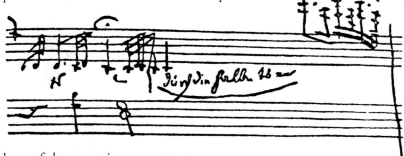

leave of absence, using as a pretext the imminent visit of Joseph II to the city: All members of the archbishop's court orchestra were required to be present. A third application met with a third refusal. Although Colloredo had taken less and less notice of his concertmaster, other than to use him as a concert performer, he was reluctant to let him leave.

Finally Mozart could bear it no longer. On 1 August 1777 he resigned. The archbishop's response was swift. On 28 August it was decreed that both father and son were free to seek their fortune elsewhere. Once freed, however, the prospect of financial insecurity alarmed Leopold, who was beginning to feel his age; he gave in and decided to stay. But on 23 September, Mozart, with his mother, bade Salzburg farewell once again.

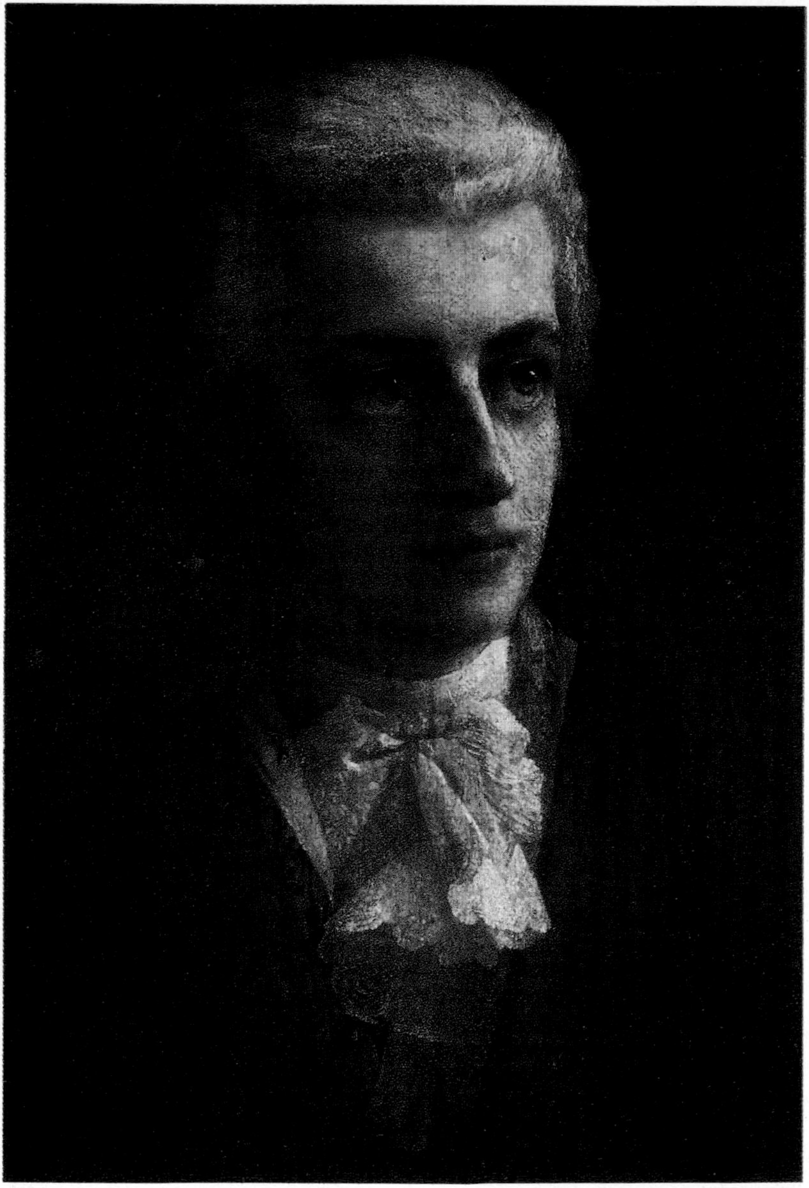

Mozart could breathe again. He had struggled free of the pressures, the boredom, and the tyrannical restrictions imposed by those who desired to control the music he wrote. His pulse quickening with hope, he set off for Munich, sure that his genius was about to be acknowledged by the world at large. He was twenty-one—still young enough to have illusions.

CHAPTER IV
DISILLUSIONMENT

" I am always in my best humour, for my heart has been as light as a feather ever since I got away from all that petty scheming! **"**

Mozart
26 September 1777

Right: An 18th-century German engraving. Opposite: An 18th-century portrait of Mozart.

On 23 September 1777 Leopold Mozart was left at home in Salzburg with the watchful Nannerl while his wife and son departed for what would be a prolonged absence. "After you had both left, I walked up our stairs very wearily and threw myself down in a chair. When we said good-bye, I had made great efforts to control myself in order not to make our parting more painful.... I was astonished how Nannerl wept, and I had the greatest difficulty in consoling her.... We played piquet [a card game] and then had supper in my room and...with God's blessing, went to bed. That is how we spent the sad day that I never thought I should have to face" (Leopold Mozart, 25 September 1777). But Mozart was in such high spirits that it was useless to attempt to conceal his delight at getting away from "the Mufti" (Colloredo)—so much so that Leopold had to caution him: "My dear Wolfgang, I beg you not to write any more jokes about our Mufti. Remember that I am in Salzburg and that one of your letters might get lost or find its way into the wrong hands."

Above: "Allerliebster Papa!," Mozart's greeting to his "dearest papa" in a letter of 1777. In that year, Leopold Mozart (right) was fifty-eight, and his career was more or less over. He would spend his remaining years in Salzburg, never quite realizing his aspirations. As a crowning irony, the *Toy* Symphony, his most enduringly popular work, was long attributed to Joseph Haydn.

By 24 September the travelers had reached Munich. Fortified by his reputation and the success he had had there three years earlier with *La Finta Giardiniera*, Mozart renewed his contacts with members of the nobility and also sought out the bishop of Chiemsee, Prince von Zeil, who was in charge of the theaters. He even had the opportunity of meeting Maximilian III in person, thanks to a cellist friend who arranged a "chance" encounter.

Munich viewed from the west in the mid-19th century. Left of center, the domed Theatine Church; right, the twin-towered Frauenkirche.

Mozart Learned a Hard Lesson: Never Antagonize a Prince

It was all in vain. Word that he had been dissatisfied

" Dearest Papa, I cannot write in verse, for I am no poet. I cannot arrange words and phrases artistically so as to produce effects of light and shade, for I am no painter. Even by signs and gestures I cannot express my thoughts and feelings, for I am no dancer. But I can do so through sounds, for I am a composer. "

Mozart
8 November 1777

with his former patron, the archbishop, had already reached the ears of Maximilian; etiquette forbade that the elector should take the side of a servant, and he had no wish to quarrel with an influential neighbor. Mozart drew the ruler's attention to his credentials, but Maximilian knew them perfectly well already: Indeed, it was he who had recommended to Mozart that he should go and make his name in Italy before looking for any permanent post.

Wolfgang was naive. Leopold, so experienced in the ways of the court, proffered advice, but his son refused to think about who or what might be useful to him and advance his cause. Some of his friends,

Mozart's exquisite lightness of touch is the result of a perfect balance between brilliant inventiveness and disciplined expression. He was totally free of the clichéd superficiality found in some 18th-century art, such as Jean-Honoré Fragonard's *The Swing* (above). Mozart's delightful creations are never without a shadow of melancholy.

such as Franz Joseph Albert, an innkeeper and an enthusiastic organizer of concerts, would have liked to keep him in Munich: Albert was even prepared to pay him an allowance until he obtained employment —an offer that wounded Leopold's paternal pride. Mozart thought he might contribute to the rebirth of German opera, in a country currently saturated with Italian. He ran into Josef Mysliveček, a composer he had met in Bologna in 1770, who tried to persuade him to return to Italy. But he did nothing decisive. Finally Leopold wrote a stern letter from Salzburg that brought Wolfgang to his senses. He and his mother moved on to Mannheim, stopping briefly at Augsburg on the way.

M ozart's cousin Maria Anna Thekla Mozart (below). In one of his whimsical letters to her, an ink blot is surrounded by the word for "pig" in four languages.

The Staid City of Augsburg Quickly Discouraged Mozart

Augsburg was where Leopold Mozart's family came from, but it had little to offer his son. An independent city, it was populated by well-to-do, long-established citizens; even its musicians were people of a certain social standing.

Mozart found an unexpected ally to share in his mockery of the Augsburg bourgeoisie—his cousin Maria Anna Thekla, daughter of his bookbinder uncle. She was as irreverent as he, and the two struck up a gleeful friendship. It was to her that he would address some of his crudest letters, whose unsubtle scatological humor deeply troubles his more fastidious admirers and puzzles many Mozart scholars.

"On the morning of this day, the 17th, I write and declare that our little cousin is beautiful, intelligent, charming, clever and gay; and that is because she has mixed with people a great deal, and has also spent some time in Munich.... Indeed we two get on extremely well, for, like myself, she is slightly wicked. We make fun of everyone together and laugh a lot."

Mozart
17 October 1777

However, in Augsburg he had another meeting with Johann Andreas Stein, the eminent piano builder whose pianos and organs he had so admired on his first visit. And the delightful hours spent at the console in St. Ulrich's Church eventually obliterated from his mind the smugness of the rich merchants who had earlier been the butt of his irony. He even agreed to appear at a society recital on 22 October. But, at the last moment, he almost refused to go on because the mayor's son made fun of the Golden Spur insignia that, on Leopold's insistent advice, he had put on for the occasion. To add insult to injury, the concert was poorly attended. Memories of his lukewarm reception in Augsburg in 1763 were revived, and he left as soon as he could.

Philippe Mercier's *A Music Party*, from around 1740 (top). Illustrations of a bow (above) and violin (right) from Denis Diderot and Jean Le Rond d'Alembert's *Encyclopédie*, 1751–80.

30 October 1777: Mozart and His Mother Arrived in Mannheim, a Musical Treasure House

The city presided over by Elector Karl Theodor possessed extraordinary musical riches, some of which are still being rediscovered today. Initiated by violinist and composer Johann Stamitz in the 1740s, there had developed in Mannheim a powerful musical impetus of both an aesthetic and a practical kind: The players in the court orchestra were of an exceptionally high caliber. Its influence was felt throughout 18th-century Europe and played an important role in laying the foundations of the classical symphony.

In the stimulating milieu of Mannheim, freed from worry about his past or his reputation, Mozart experienced a rebirth. His genius was finally being recognized by some of the foremost musicians in Europe. They gave him not only friendship, but guidance, which was both competent and much appreciated. While there were those who found him too impetuous, Mozart paid little heed to their remonstrances.

Karl Theodor, whose reign had begun in 1749, was an ardent patron

Karl Theodor (1724–99, above), elector of Bavaria, was a passionate patron of the arts and sciences. He had close ties with Voltaire in France as well as with leading German scholars. In 1775 he founded a society for the safeguarding of German language and literature.

of the arts and sciences. He had been much influenced by French fashions and first sought at his court to emulate Versailles, but then he decided instead to champion a return to a national culture. The German national theater that he founded was inexpressibly exciting for Mozart. His encounter with Karl Theodor on 6 November after a concert was cordial enough for Mozart tò hope for a new opera commission; during their conversation he made calculated suggestions about the elector's children's musical education and hinted about his desire to stay in Mannheim, hoping to be offered a position.

But the days passed, and no message came from the court. Money began to run out, Leopold became anxious, and there was a voluminous exchange of letters. Leopold's became agitated: "Not a word about where you are going or what plans you may be making.... The object of your journey...was and is and must be to obtain an appointment or to earn some money.... You, however, seem to think nothing matters" (27 November 1777).

Karl Theodor's reply finally came; it was negative. But Mozart stayed on in Mannheim. He felt so at home there and was composing so happily that he simply ignored his money problems. The death of Maximilian III late in the year came as a jolt: Karl Theodor succeeded him as elector and moved with his entourage to Munich.

In January 1778 a happy opportunity presented itself during a brief visit to the Princess of Orange at Kirchheim-Bolanden. Mozart wrote to his father on 17 January: "I shall get eight louis d'or at least, for, since she is extremely fond of singing, I have had four arias copied for her; and, since she has a nice little orchestra and gives a concert every day, I shall also present her with a symphony. The copying of the arias will not cost me much, for it has been done by a certain Herr Weber, who will go there with me. I don't know whether I have already written about his daughter or not—she sings really most admirably...."

Aloysia Weber (below, in a 1784 engraving) was a coloratura soprano. Mozart wrote the concert aria "Popoli di Tessaglia" ("People of Thessaly") for her.

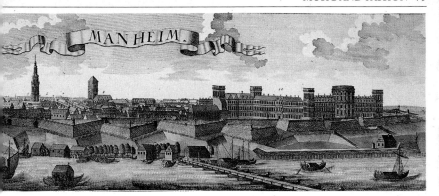

Mozart Had Just Turned Twenty-Two; Aloysia Weber Was Eighteen

Mozart had fallen madly in love with the young singer. He desired more and more to write an opera, one that would draw attention to his new beloved. He was quite incapable of withholding from his father the news of his dawning passion and his hopes for the future. Leopold was aghast. Aloysia's father, Fridolin Weber, was only a lowly copyist and member of the chorus at the court theater. To Leopold, who was concerned about respectability and cherished social ambitions for his son, a match with Weber's daughter seemed disastrous.

Leopold resorted to emotional blackmail, pointing out that he was getting old, that Nannerl was sacrificing her own career giving lessons in order to finance the household, and that Wolfgang's travels were simply getting the family into debt. Would Wolfgang give in to his father's arguments and obvious distress?

It seems that Mozart did pay heed, though without giving up his love or his creative ambitions. He consented to go to Paris, after presenting his Mannheim friends and Aloysia with several more arias and ariettas.

Mozart and his mother set off for Paris on 13 March 1778. The journey took nine and a half days.

Mannheim in the early 18th century. The vast electoral palace can be seen at right. It was during the reign of Karl Philipp, Karl Theodor's father, that Mannheim made a determined effort to emancipate itself from the influence of Italy and become a musical center in its own right. Between 1745 and 1777, its complement of singers and instrumentalists virtually doubled. The Mannheim musicians were fine players and often composers, too. They excelled in performing *sinfonie concertanti* (in which a group of solo instruments is set off against a larger orchestra), the genre that was their particular specialty.

"We really thought that we should not be able to endure it," wrote Mozart on 23 March 1778, "for never in my life have I been so bored." Anna Maria was dejected. She missed Salzburg and sensed that her son was only putting up with her presence instead of being glad of it. She was apprehensive of finding herself in a foreign country of whose language she knew not a word. As for Mozart, he was meditating on the advice about his career offered by his Parisian friend Baron Grimm in response to an appeal from Leopold.

Mozart Was Forced to Take Pupils in Order to Survive in Paris

Mozart had already eloquently expressed what he felt about giving lessons. "I will gladly give lessons as a favour, especially when I see that my pupil has

Fragonard's *The Music Lesson,* from about 1755.

It is hard to imagine Mozart teaching. In his correspondence he admits to an aversion for an occupation he considered unbearably boring unless the pupil was very gifted; but worse than that, he felt that it should be left to those who could do nothing else. He realized that he was a genius, that genius could not be taught, and that time was too precious to waste.

talent, inclination, and a desire to learn; but to be forced to go to a house at a particular hour, or to have to wait at home for a pupil—that is something I cannot do, no matter how much money I might earn. … I neither can nor should bury in this way the talent for composition with which God in his goodness has so richly endowed me" (letter of 7 February 1778). But now he had no choice.

The first days in Paris were disagreeable. The Mozarts were housed in a sordid lodging where it was impossible to bring a keyboard instrument up the stairs. But Baron Grimm undertook to introduce the young man into some good houses; and some of Mozart's musician friends from Mannheim were visiting Paris, too.

Soon Anna Maria's letters to her husband took on a more positive tone. They had found decent lodgings, and Mozart had been able to meet several influential people in the Parisian world of music. He had also been presented to the Count of Guines, who was in favor at court; Mozart wrote the famous Concerto for Flute and Harp (K. 299) for the count and his daughter, who had become one of his pupils.

These moments of satisfaction had to compensate for others that were just the opposite, such as the occasion when he was invited to visit a duchess, treated with a politeness akin to extreme disdain, kept waiting in an icy-cold room, and then made to play

A quartet formed by a tiny *violino piccolo*, harp, flute, and horn, in a mid-18th-century painting by Pierre Antoine Baudouin. The harp in use in Mozart's time was not the modern concert double-action harp, which was perfected by Sébastien Erard in the early 19th century, but the pedal harp. The instrument had seven pedals, each corresponding to a note of the scale. This is the kind of harp for which Mozart wrote the concerto K. 299, in which the instrument's crystalline notes are joined by an ideal partner, the flute.

on a badly tuned piano while the assembled company occupied itself sketching.

There were other disappointments. The score of a sinfonia concertante, which was to be premiered at a concert by some of Mozart's Mannheim acquaintances, was not even copied out for the instrumentalists and thus has never been performed. Whatever the reason—perhaps a deliberate attempt by a competing composer to frustrate Mozart, perhaps only negligence on the part of concert director Jean Le Gros—it is a pity that this work in which French taste blended with the spirit of Mannheim has been lost.

In the midst of all these contretemps—whose influence can be heard in anguished moments in the Piano Sonata no. 8 (K. 310), also composed at this time— Le Gros commissioned a symphony, perhaps to make amends. Symphony no. 31 (K. 297), the *Paris*, performed on 18 June for a dazzled audience, is like a burst of sunshine.

But in the end, Paris turned its back on Mozart. All he was offered in the way of employment was the post of organist at Versailles, a position that did not interest him. He detested the French capital, declaring it too capricious and subject to the whims of fashion.

Left: Wind instruments, from Diderot and d'Alembert's *Encyclopédie*. The Sinfonia Concertante K. 297b was originally intended for flute, oboe, bassoon, and horn. But the revised version specifies instead of the flute the clarinet—a new instrument that Mozart loved. He hated the flute, and claimed that writing for instruments he hated made him numb.

Tragedy Strikes

In the middle of June 1778, Anna Maria's delicate health began to decline; she was quickly struck down by a fever, fell into a coma, and died on 3 July. Mozart's grief and sense of isolation were profound, though his sense of propriety led him to conceal these emotions beneath a mask of resignation. But at the same time, finally freed from a parental vigilance he found oppressive, he began to feel more enterprising. Although Aloysia was still present in his thoughts, he considered extending his stay in Paris in the hope of obtaining a commission for an opera.

But he had misjudged Leopold and Grimm: The two had continued to correspond, and Leopold accepted everything the baron said without question;

Below: A late-18th-century drawing of the church and cemetery of the Holy Innocents in Paris, where Mozart's mother's funeral took place. "By the mercy of God I have borne it all with fortitude and composure. When her illness became dangerous I prayed to God for two things only —a happy death for her, and strength and courage for myself" (Mozart, letter of 3 July 1778).

Mozart had had to borrow money from Grimm, his patron in Paris, and was now reminded in no uncertain terms of his debt. Furthermore, he had offended Grimm by refusing to side with the supporters of Piccinni against Gluck in a Parisian musical feud.

Mozart was somewhat consoled at the beginning of August by a visit from his friend Johann Christian Bach. But his father was putting increased pressure on him in a final bid to get him to return to Salzburg. Leopold renewed his entreaties to Karl Theodor and even appealed to Padre Martini for help. The Salzburg organist Adlgasser and the Kapellmeister Joseph Lolli had both died; now, Leopold felt, was the chance for his son to obtain a permanent prestigious post. Colloredo agreed, even promising Mozart a leave of absence to honor any contracts or commissions he might be offered.

Mozart thought that if he refused, he might cause the death of his father and inherit all his debts. If he accepted, he believed there was a chance that Aloysia might come to Salzburg, too, and try her luck at court.

Full of Dread, Mozart Reluctantly Agreed to Return to Salzburg

On 26 September Grimm arranged for a carriage to take Mozart to Strasbourg, where he was to give three concerts. On 29 September he arrived—in Mannheim, on an unexpected detour to Aloysia's hometown. But Aloysia had just taken a position in Munich; Wolfgang followed her there, and the longed-for reunion took place in Munich on Christmas Day. When he had last seen her nine months earlier she had been a young singer just starting out; now she was an established soprano, whose only thoughts were for her career. Mozart received a cruel rebuff. His parting gift to her, however, the concert aria "Popoli di Tessaglia" ("People of Thessaly"), was nonetheless splendid—a vehicle to

Nannerl, Wolfgang, and Leopold Mozart in 1781, with the dead Anna Maria present in the form of her portrait.

display her voice to the best possible advantage.

After presenting the electress of Bavaria with the violin sonatas K. 301–6, there was nothing for Mozart to do but continue his return journey, accompanied by his cousin, Maria Anna Thekla. On 16 January 1779, after a separation of fifteen months, Mozart was reunited with his father and sister in Salzburg. But it was a melancholy occasion, for Anna Maria Mozart lay buried in France.

"If your mother had come back home from Mannheim, she would not have died.... You would have got to Paris at a better time...and my poor wife would still be [alive] in Salzburg."
Leopold Mozart
27 August 1778

Mozart had given up the struggle and resigned himself to suffering the vexing Colloredo. But his creativity had been enhanced by his contact with Italian, German, and French music, and he knew, even if the public still did not, that he was an unrivaled genius.

CHAPTER V
"MY HAPPINESS IS JUST BEGINNING"

Mozart, in a late-19th-century painting (opposite).

A musical trio in an 18th-century silhouette (above).

On 17 January 1779, just ten days before his twenty-third birthday, Mozart took up his post as official organist and composer to the archbishop of Salzburg. His return had been sad: He found the everyday routine to be tedious, and he disliked being obliged to supply works to order (among which, in March, was the *Coronation Mass*). But, happily, a diversion appeared in the form of a traveling theatrical company. Opera came once again to the fore. For this company, Mozart made *La Finta Giardiniera* into a singspiel, a type of German comic opera in which arias and folk songs alternate with spoken dialogue. Another singspiel, *Zaïde ou le Sérail* (*Zaïde, or the Seraglio*), remained unfinished but was the inspiration for *Die Entführung aus dem Serail* (*The Abduction from the Seraglio*), which he began a few months later. This troupe was soon followed by another, this one led by Emanuel Schikaneder (1751–1812), future librettist of *The Magic Flute*.

Mozart, Desperately Bored, Almost Lost the Will to Compose

The joys of the theater broke the monotony and introduced him to the works of Shakespeare and contemporary French and German playwrights. And Leopold seemed happy to have him around. But Mozart wrote little. Among his better works at this time were the Symphony no. 33 (K. 319), his second symphony since 1774, and the unique Serenade K. 230, featuring the merry calls of the post horn (the horn used by mail coach guards in the 18th century), which give it its nickname. Best of all was the Sinfonia Concertante for Violin and Viola (K. 364), a grandiose work of extraordinary expressive power, written in the summer of 1779. But the following months saw virtually no compositions: Mozart's next work, the Symphony no. 34 (K. 338), is dated 29 August 1780. Either he had a temporary block or he was declining to compose in the genres demanded by his job and the tastes of the Salzburg public.

The second half of the 18th century saw the height of the vogue for concertos and *sinfonie concertanti*; both offered opportunities for felicitous combinations of contrasting instruments. Keyboard and violin were especially favored, but the oboe, trumpet, and clarinet were also popular. Mozart wrote four concertos for the horn, all dedicated to his friend Ignaz Leutgeb, horn player and

cheesemonger. The horn's solemn yet warm tone is a favorite with audiences, although it is perhaps the most difficult of all instruments to master. In this 18th-century group portrait of instruments (opposite), horns share a sort of cozy domesticity with a violin, a recorder, and a cello.

Above: An 18th-century illustration of a hunting horn.

At the Violin Maker's

Aview of an imaginary 18th-century musical instrument workshop. The violin as we know it was perfected in Italy during the 17th and 18th centuries by Nicolò Amati (1596–1684) and his pupils, of whom the best known are Antonio Stradivari and Giuseppe Antonio Guarneri. Earlier popular stringed instruments were viols, held on or between the legs (hence the term "viola da gamba"), and fiddles, held on the arm and often used to accompany folk dancing. The violin gained supremacy at the end of the 17th century as one of the most prestigious solo instruments.

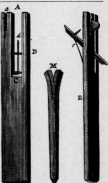

Keyboard Instruments

Square, or table, piano (above left); harpsichord (below left); and spinet (below right). Originating in the 14th century, the harpsichord strongly influenced the development of musical form in Europe. The spinet, which became common in the 16th century, is smaller and quieter, and its strings often run diagonally to the keyboard. In both instruments the strings are plucked by a leather or quill plectrum attached to a pivoting tongue in a jack (examples above). The harpsichord and the spinet were superseded by the piano, developed in the 18th century. Because the strings of a piano are struck by hammers rather than plucked, volume can be subtly varied. Thus, the melody could be brought out in relation to the accompaniment, and passages could grow gradually louder or softer.

IDOMENEO.
DRAMMA
PER
MUSICA
DA RAPPRESENTARSI
NEL TEATRO NUOVO DI
CORTE
PER COMANDO
DI S.A.S.E.
CARLO TEODORO
Come Palatino del Rheno, Duca dell'
alta, e bassa Baviera, e del Palatinato
Superiore, etc. etc. Archidapifero,
ed Elettore, etc. etc.
NEL CARNOVALE
1781.

La Poesia è del Signor Abate Gianbattista Varesco
Capellano di Corte di S. A. R. l Arcivescovo, e Principe di Salisburgo.
La Musica è del Signor Maestro Wolfgango Amadeo Mozart Academico di Bologna, e di Verona, in fin attual servizio di S. A. R. l Arcivescovo, e Principe di Salisburgo.
La Traduzione è del Signor Andrea Schachtner, pure in attual servizio di S. A. R. l'Arcivescovo, e Principe di Salisburgo.

MONACO.
Appresso Francesco Giuseppe Thuille.

At Last, the Chance to Write a Full-Scale Grand Opera

In the summer of 1780, Karl Theodor, now installed in Munich as elector of Bavaria, asked Mozart to compose an opera seria for the upcoming carnival season. The chosen libretto, *Idomeneo, Rè di Creta* (*Idomeneo, King of Crete*), bore the signature of the Salzburg court chaplain, Gianbattista Varesco. Colloredo, unable to resist this double honor, granted his organist a leave of absence.

Meanwhile, the Weber family had moved to Vienna to be with Aloysia, but many other old friends of Mozart's were still in Munich. Surrounded by affection, Mozart responded with a particularly frenzied burst of creative activity: "My head and my hands are so full of Act III that it would be no wonder if I were to turn into a third act myself" (letter of 3 January 1781).

When the Empress Maria Theresa died that winter, Colloredo had to go to Vienna for the funeral and the accession of Joseph II. Leopold and Nannerl took advantage of his absence to attend the premiere of *Idomeneo* in Munich on 29 January 1781. It was a triumph, but a short-lived one. People found the music baffling: It broke the rigid conventions of opera seria by giving the protagonists real emotions and individuality. But Mozart was pleased.

On 12 March, however, Colloredo summoned him to

The genre of opera seria reached its peak in the 18th century. The action was advanced by recitatives and slowed by arias expressing the emotions of the characters, usually heroes from mythology or classical antiquity. Much emphasis was put on moral virtues in these highly artificial and formal texts. In an 18th-century painting from the school of Pietro Longhi (opposite), we see a typical scene in a Venetian opera house. Left: Frontispiece for original libretto of *Idomeneo.* Below: A portrait of Mozart.

Above: Mozart at work.

Vienna. Their relationship quickly degenerated into open hostility. Flushed by his recent success, Mozart would no longer tolerate being treated like a servant; he had after all made some headway in aristocratic circles. It irked him to be reduced to the same level as other employees of the archbishop.

Animosity Began to Boil Over, to Mozart's Delight

Colloredo's motives are inscrutable. Perhaps he felt that his rebellious employee's presence upset the rest of the court orchestra, and he wanted to keep him in his place. Certainly he provoked Mozart's hostility by attempting (in vain) to prevent him from taking part in a charity concert for the benefit of the widows and orphans of musicians.

By now, Mozart had realized that it would be in his best interest to stay in Vienna. His recent success, his relationships with members of the aristocracy, the

" I have here [in Vienna] the finest and most useful acquaintances in the world.... All possible honour is shown me and I am paid into the bargain. So why expect me to languish in Salzburg for the sake of 400 gulden, hanging about being no use to anyone, being neither properly paid nor encouraged?...What would be the end of it?"
Mozart to his father
12 May 1781

presence of good friends—he began to believe that he could earn his living in the capital, especially after he learned that the superintendent of the German national theater in Vienna, Gottlieb Stephanie, was thinking of asking him for an opera.

So he waited for the rupture; he even longed for it, to Leopold's alarm. It came soon enough. In Mozart's partly encoded letter of 9 May to his father he relates in detail the stormy interview that led to his dismissal, sparing no detail of the abuse that the archbishop, beside himself with rage, heaped on him. His letter ends, "Now please be cheerful, for my happiness is just beginning, and I trust that my happiness will be yours also.... I want nothing more to do with Salzburg." Was this the first time that a composer put his art above all else—refusing the security of servitude and opting for liberty?

It took another month to be sure of his freedom, for Leopold attempted to intervene, asking the archbishop's chief steward, Count Arco, for assistance. The count lectured the defiant Mozart on how to behave: He was later to be proved right on some points, such as when he warned the composer against the fickleness and frivolity of the Viennese. He finished his diatribe, as is well known, by kicking the young man out of the room. Mozart turned his back on Salzburg and settled down in Vienna.

Independence Did Not Come Cheaply: Mozart Found Himself Penniless in Vienna

Starting in May he lodged with the Webers. Aloysia was now married, and Wolfgang's thoughts had not

A view of the Domgasse in Vienna, where Mozart composed *The Marriage of Figaro*.

" You must be patient for a little while longer and then I shall be able to prove to you how useful Vienna is going to be to us all.... When I am in Salzburg I long for a hundred amusements, but here not for a single one. For just to be in Vienna is in itself entertainment enough. "
Mozart to his father
26 May 1781

yet turned to her sister Constanze; he was just a lodger like anyone else.

Little by little his life began to get organized. He took one pupil, a countess, and began an appeal for the publication of four violin sonatas, K. 376, 377, 379, and 380. But it was summertime, and musical activity was limited.

The theater threw him a lifeline: Gottlieb Stephanie confirmed the commission for *The Abduction from the Seraglio*.

At last Mozart would write a German opera and thus participate in the revival of national art desired by Joseph II. It took a year to turn the dream into reality, and meanwhile his relationship with Leopold was strained almost to the breaking point.

Constanze Weber Entered the Scene

Gossip travels fast, and Leopold soon heard that his son was interested in Aloysia's younger sister, Constanze. A warm affection had sprung up between Mozart and the younger Weber, though he claimed he was not really in love with her. Pressured by Johann Thorwart, the Weber girls' guardian since the death of their father, and by their mother, Mozart agreed to an engagement, partly to remove Constanze from an unhappy home. He justified his decision to his father in a letter of 15 December 1781, "She is not witty, but she has enough sound common sense to be able to fulfil her duties as a wife and mother."

The Seraglio was not progressing, and Mozart was not composing much else. He had hopes for a position at court as a tutor,

Left: Antonio Salieri, appointed court composer in Vienna in 1774, was truly not a serious rival, though his scheming against the production of *Così Fan Tutte* in 1790 was worrisome for Mozart.

Opposite: Mozart playing before Joseph II at Schönbrunn, as imagined in a 19th-century engraving. The emperor is unlikely to have listened with such respectful concentration.

Below: Mozart and the singer Catarina Cavalieri. He wrote the part of Constanze in *The Seraglio* for her and added the aria "Mi tradì" when she sang the role of Elvira in the Vienna premiere of *Don Giovanni* in August 1789.

but he was passed over in favor of Antonio Salieri (1750–1825), an Italian composer. Soon, however, a piano contest with Muzio Clementi (1752–1832), in which he was able to outshine the virtuoso composer, enhanced his reputation and gave him new optimism. Among his pupils now were the wife of a rich publisher and two countesses. The income from their lessons was enough to live on. Leopold continued to write bitterly reproachful letters, which the prospect of a marriage did nothing to improve. Yet Mozart still wished sincerely for his father's blessing.

" This piece [*The Seraglio*] seems to me to epitomize the happy days of youth, whose flowering, once over, can never be recaptured. "
Carl Maria von Weber
1818

In 1782 All Practicalities Were Forgotten as Mozart Discovered Johann Sebastian Bach (1685–1750)

The big event in Mozart's musical life at this time came when Baron Gottfried van Swieten introduced him to the works of Handel and particularly Johann Sebastian Bach. (Bach's son Johann Christian, Mozart's old friend, had just died.) Mozart was so enraptured by the beauty and complexity of the elder Bach's works that he transcribed fugues from the *Well-Tempered Clavier*, a collection of forty-eight preludes and fugues, for the baron's orchestra and also improvised some preludes.

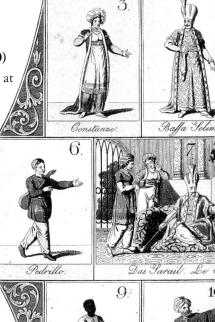

During the summer Mozart was involved in a series of Sunday open-air concerts held in some of Vienna's handsome squares; Archduke Maximilian honored the opening concert with his presence.

But of course it was *The Seraglio* that occupied most of Mozart's time until the end of May. The premiere took place on 16

July. Joseph II's reaction was guarded. "Too many notes, dear Mozart," he is reputed to have said, though he should have shown himself receptive to the opera's themes of tolerance and generosity enhanced by a score that scintillated with the exuberance of youth and exalted liberty and love. The public was ecstatic. *The Seraglio* was given sixteen performances within a few months. "My opera was presented yesterday for the third time … to the greatest applause; and again, in spite of the dreadful heat, the theatre was packed…. I may say that people are quite mad about this opera. It really does one good to be so applauded" (letter of 27 July 1782).

Belmonte.

Blonde.

The heroine with whom the opera's characters Belmonte and Pasha Selim are in love is called Constanze, but it would be a mistake to seize on this coincidence too readily. The real-life couple had just gone through a difficult time. Frau Weber had forced her future son-in-law to sign a contract committing him to pay her daughter 300 florins a year if he broke the engagement. Constanze immediately tore up the document, but the unpleasant memory remained.

Mozart Married Constanze

The couple was married on 4 August 1782 in St. Stephen's Cathedral. Leopold's blessing did not arrive until

Engravings (center) of the characters and silhouettes (below) of the leading singers in the Vienna premiere of *The Abduction from the Seraglio*. There are five sung roles, a spoken one, and two parts for actors.

Therese Teyber

Valent Adamberger

Catarina Cavalieri

Ernst Dauer

the next day. Wolfgang had just finished Symphony no. 35 (K. 385), the *Haffner*, another commission from the Haffner family, but his prospects were still uncertain; no gesture came from Joseph II and his court, and he briefly considered trying his luck in France or England. Constanze found that she was pregnant. Then the summer was over, and the lessons and concerts resumed. Three more piano concertos appeared, Nos. 11, 12, and 13 (K. 413–5). "These concertos are a happy medium between being too easy and too difficult," wrote Mozart to his father on 28 December 1782. "They are very brilliant, pleasing to the ear, and natural, without being vapid. There are passages here and there from which only connoisseurs can derive satisfaction; but these passages are written in such a way that non-connoisseurs will find them satisfying too, without knowing why." But he expressed a more intimate side of himself in the String Quartet K. 387, the first of the set of six he dedicated to Joseph Haydn.

St. Stephen's Cathedral, in Vienna. Here Mozart and Constanze were married on 4 August 1782. In 1791 Mozart secured from the municipality the title of unpaid assistant to Leopold Hoffmann, Kapellmeister at St. Stephen's, with the assurance that he would succeed to the post when the incumbent died.

Constanze Mozart, in a portrait dated 1802. A reappraisal of Constanze has taken place in recent years, challenging the traditional disparaging view that she was extravagant and careless. Much documentary evidence seems to reveal that she was competent at handling financial affairs and a tireless champion of her husband's music. An obituary of Mozart reported that Constanze was "a good mother to the two surviving children born of their union and an entirely worthy wife who sought to prevent Mozart from falling victim to his own excesses and unwise decisions."

The year 1783 began in a mood of elation natural to a young couple (he was twenty-seven, she was nineteen) expecting their first baby. The lessons and concerts were bringing in a sufficient income, and the only slight disappointment was the closing of the German opera company, which meant that the Italians, openly led by Salieri, were back in the fore.

In March Mozart met Lorenzo da Ponte, a former priest who had been unfrocked for immoral conduct. The encounter would soon change his musical life. But first, Wolfgang wanted to bring his new wife to Salzburg to meet his father and sister. Mozart's last visit to his native city lasted three months. It was an awkward, uneasy time for Constanze and also for her husband, who was technically still in the employ of Colloredo, since no document existed that could prove otherwise. The couple had not brought Raimund Leopold, their "fine sturdy baby, round as a ball," who had been born on 17 June while his father was busy finishing the second of the "Haydn" quartets (K. 421). During the three months in Salzburg, Mozart wrote the duos for violin and viola K. 423–4 and also arranged a performance of his incomplete Mass in C minor (K. 427).

The Mozarts had no wish to prolong their Salzburg stay; the three months were up at the end of October. They returned via Linz, where Mozart composed his Symphony no. 36 (K. 425) in four days to thank Count Thun for his hospitality. News of a calamity awaited them on their return to Vienna: Their baby was dead.

Vienna Continued to Treat Mozart Well in 1784

Despite his grief, Mozart remained buoyant. He wrote four more piano concertos, two for his talented new pupil Babette Ployer (No. 14, K. 449, and No. 17, K. 453) and two whirlwind ones for himself to play (No. 15, K. 450, and No. 16, K. 451). Time flew by; it was summer, and another baby was expected soon. In Salzburg Nannerl married at last, into the minor aristocracy—a baron. She never saw her brother again.

On 21 September Wolfgang and Constanze's second son, Karl Thomas, was born. The winter season got under way, with a concert series that constantly required new compositions, but there was also time for friends and chamber music sessions: Karl Ditter von Dittersdorf and Joseph Haydn played the violins, Mozart the viola, and Johann Baptist

A string quartet session. Mozart wrote twenty-three quartets between 1770 and 1790.

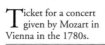

Ticket for a concert given by Mozart in Vienna in the 1780s.

Vanhal the cello. These were favorite moments for Mozart, who was also just finishing the six quartets dedicated to Haydn that he had begun in 1782.

1785: An Exceptionally Productive Year

In the midst of all this creativity, Mozart made an important decision, the result of long reflection: On 14 December 1784 he became a member of the Freemasons, a fraternal organization of liberal intellectuals. February 1785 brought a surprise visit from Leopold, who was moved to tears when Haydn declared that his son was the greatest composer he knew. Leopold's arrival coincided with the completion of the tragic Piano Concerto no. 20 (K. 466), followed immediately by the radiant Piano Concerto no. 21 (K. 467).

Mozart's friend soprano Nancy Storace (1765–1817), the first to sing Susanna in *The Marriage of Figaro*.

A meeting of a Masonic lodge in Vienna, 1790; the figure at the far right has been identified as Mozart. The Masonic hierarchy dictates three degrees for the spiritual progress of the society's members: Apprentice, Fellow, and Master. Each degree has its own visual symbols. Mozart progressed rapidly up the hierarchy, though the date when he became a Master is not known. Freemasonry imposed certain rules and duties on its members. The influence of Masonic thought, especially the ideals of brotherhood and charity, is clear in Mozart's later works, which also contain a wealth of Masonic symbolism. For example, his first Masonic song, *Zur Gesellenreise* (*The Companions' Journey*, K. 468), written in 1785, probably for the ceremony marking his promotion to the second degree, is written with two flats; pieces referring to Master Masons, such as the cantata *Die Maurerfreude* (*The Masons' Joy*, K. 471), are written with three flats; Apprenticeship is symbolized by the key of F, which has only one flat.

Of course Wolfgang had not forgotten about opera, but he had yet to find a new libretto. Da Ponte had proposed *Lo Sposo Deluso* (*The Deluded Spouse*) but had only jotted down a few ideas. A German opera was out of the question for the moment.

Then Mozart heard of a seditious comedy that had recently caused a furor in Paris: It was called *The Marriage of Figaro,* by Pierre Augustin Caron de Beaumarchais. Emperor Joseph had banned it from the national theater in Vienna, but Mozart, attracted by the subject matter—it was the sequel to *The Barber of Seville,* an operatic version of which was a proven success—suggested it to Da Ponte, who promised to persuade Joseph to change his mind. Mozart worked on the opera during the latter part of the year, in the meantime producing another piano concerto (No. 22, K. 482). He had to keep the money coming in: The Mozarts' financial situation seemed to be getting worse. In response to a request from the emperor he also wrote a one-act singspiel, *Der Schauspieldirektor* (*The Impresario*), which was performed at Schönbrunn palace on 7 February 1786 in an evening that also included Salieri's *Prima la Musica e Poi le Parole* (*First the Music, then the Words*).

The humanity and wit of *The Marriage of Figaro* have made it one of the most perennially popular of all operas. Mozart wrote most of it in a house on the Domgasse, a street in Vienna (left). Right: The set for Act IV, by Hans Frahm. Below: 19th-century costumes for the characters Cherubino and Susanna.

At the Age of Thirty, Mozart Began to Feel His Artistic Isolation

Two more piano concertos—No. 23 (K. 488) and the lesser-known but magnificent No. 24

(K. 491)—appeared in March. And then, on 1 May 1786, came the premiere of *The Marriage of Figaro*. It was only a qualified success. Some members of the audience were wildly enthusiastic, but others were not, for the audacity of the dramatic situations and the originality of the music did not appeal to Vienna's unsophisticated public.

Mozart felt misunderstood and alone. His most personal work, the remarkable string quartets dedicated to Haydn, had aroused no interest. He was sad, too, because his third son, Johann Thomas, born on 16 October, had survived only a month. The Mozarts briefly considered going to England, but finally hope came from Prague.

" Of all the performers in this opera at that time, but one survives—myself.… All the original performers had the advantage of the instruction of the composer, who transfused into their minds his inspired meaning. I never shall forget his little animated countenance, when lighted up with the glowing rays of genius—it is as impossible to describe it, as it would be to paint sun-beams.… I remember at the first rehearsal of the full band, Mozart was on the stage with his crimson pelisse and gold-laced cocked hat, giving the time of the music to the orchestra. "

Michael Kelly
Reminiscences, 1826

In 1787 Mozart was thirty-one. He would live only four more years—four years during which the financial difficulties that had dogged him for so long continued unabated. These were perhaps the darkest years of his life, yet during them he composed his most radiant masterpieces.

CHAPTER VI
LIGHT AND DARKNESS

Opposite: This unfinished, enigmatic portrait was painted in 1789–90 by Joseph Lange, Aloysia Weber's husband.

Above: A view of Prague in a mid-18th-century engraving.

The year 1787 started well. On 11 January Mozart arrived in Prague, with Constanze, to conduct *The Marriage of Figaro* at the invitation of a Count Thun. The opera was received with wild enthusiasm, and the composer was the toast of the town. He gave a concert of his Symphony no. 38 (K. 504, the *Prague*) and performed some improvisations to a hall that was full to overflowing. When Mozart returned to Vienna, he had not only the ovations of Prague resounding in his ears but a commission for a new opera from Pasquale Bondini, the director of the Prague theater, in his pocket.

The Prague Visit Was Followed by Hard Times

A group of friends visiting from England, including Nancy Storace (who sang Susanna in *The Marriage of Figaro*), had left Vienna. And the loss of another close friend reminded Mozart of the omnipresence of death; he accepted it stoically, but gave expression to his anguish in string quintets K. 515 and K. 516.

Fate began to hound him cruelly. Leopold had been ill for some time, but his sudden death on 28 May was a profound shock to his son. A door had slammed on his past. Yet he was forced to continue working, and in August he produced one of his best-loved compositions, the Serenade K. 525, *Eine Kleine Nachtmusik* (*A Little Night Music*), for a string quartet plus double bass (the largest instrument in the violin family).

The opera commissioned by Bondini made little progress during the summer. Da Ponte

It was at the home of Mozart's friends the Duscheks in Prague that he finished *Don Giovanni*. Josepha Duschek was a singer, pianist, and composer who continued to perform until well into the 19th century. It is said that she once locked Mozart into a room and refused to release him until he had written her a concert aria. This was "Bella mia fiamma, addio!" ("My beautiful love, farewell!"). Right: Mozart playing on the Duscheks' piano.

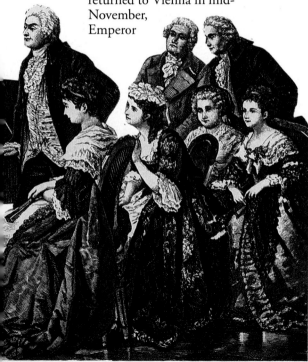

had proposed the libretto, *Don Giovanni,* one of many existing treatments of the Don Juan story, but the preparations did not run smoothly. In fact, the score was not completed until the very last minute: Legend has it that the overture was not written until two days before the first night, 29 October! Nonetheless, the opera was received with tremendous acclaim in Prague. When Mozart returned to Vienna in mid-November, Emperor

One April day there was a knock at the door of the Mozarts' humble lodgings. It was a youth of seventeen, organist for the archbishop of Cologne. His name was Ludwig van Beethoven (1770–1827). Mozart's biographer Otto Jahn described the scene (depicted at left in a late-19th-century wood engraving): "At Mozart's request Beethoven played. Mozart, guessing that it was a party piece learned by heart, was polite but unimpressed. Beethoven understood, and asked Mozart for a theme on which he could improvise freely.… He played so brilliantly that Mozart, slipping into the next room where some friends were waiting, exclaimed: 'Look out for that man; one day he'll have the world talking about him.'"

Joseph nominated him "composer of the imperial chamber," replacing Gluck, who had recently died—though the salary he offered Mozart was noticeably lower.

Mozart's Star Waned as the Viennese Public, Fickle as Ever, Lost Interest

On 27 December 1787, to Wolfgang's delight, Constanze gave birth to a daughter, Theresia. But the family's financial problems were going from bad to worse. The composer's attempt to open subscriptions to pay for a concert or the printing of a new work received no response. It is clear that he had no idea how to handle money—he tried for a short while to keep track of his accounts and to catalogue his works, but neither effort lasted. Constanze was content to live from hand to mouth, spending money when there was any and concentrating on keeping up appearances. She was almost continually pregnant, and the two went from illness to illness, barely keeping their heads above water.

In 1788 the deadly cycle of debts began in earnest. Mozart's begging letters to his friend Johann Michael Puchberg, a rich merchant and fellow Mason, are heartrending.

Vienna continued to shun him: The 7 May performance of *Don Giovanni* was a flop. Emperor Joseph II summed up the situation

Mozart and Da Ponte's *Don Giovanni* was first performed in Prague on 29 October 1787 by an Italian opera company. Zerlina (left) and Leporello (opposite below), in an early Paris production. Julius Nisle's 1941 lithographs (below and opposite above) showing Don Giovanni wooing Zerlina and the confusion at the end of Act I.

Don Juan, oder: der bestrafte Bösewicht.

at one of the final performances: "The opera is divine, I would say it is even more beautiful than *Figaro*; but it is not a meat suitable for the teeth of my Viennese." To which Mozart is said to have replied, "Give them time to chew on it!"

Summer 1788 Was a Time of Extraordinary Creativity: Mozart Challenged His Fate

Up until June, Mozart's best composition of 1788 was the brilliant Piano Concerto no. 26 (K. 537), nicknamed the *Coronation* because it was performed two years later at the coronation of Emperor Leopold II in Frankfurt (Leopold succeeded his brother Joseph). The sadness of recent years was reflected in the deeply poignant Adagio for Piano in B minor

(K. 540), written on 19 March. But in the summer Mozart produced a string of masterpieces, the first of which was the Piano Trio no. 5 in E major (K. 542), commissioned by Mozart's friend Puchberg. Next came the Divertimento for String Trio K. 563, dedicated to his friend and creditor, and then three symphonies. Symphony no. 39 in E flat (K. 543) was finished on 26 June 1788—three days before the death of his daughter. He completed the tragic No. 40 in G minor (K. 550) on 25 July and No. 41 in C (K. 551)—the superb *Jupiter* —on 10 August. One is struck by the strength of Mozart's determination to triumph over personal disaster and by his unquenchable confidence, no doubt fortified by the philosophical precepts of Freemasonry. Mozart did not give in. He fought on his own terms for what mattered to him above all else: his music.

The Next Six Months Were Devoted to Earning His Bread

The German Dances, written next for the court of Emperor Joseph II, were charming but not especially distinguished. More interesting

Emperor Joseph II died on 20 February 1790. He was succeeded by his brother Leopold II (left), formerly grand duke of Tuscany. Joseph II's wish was to be remembered as a monarch who was sensitive to the main concerns of his time and his subjects, even if it meant offending the nobility by attacking their privileges; Leopold was much more cautious and less idealistic.

were the up-to-date orchestrations of works by
Bach and Handel, a task assigned Mozart by a
nostalgic Baron van Swieten. Mozart took the score
of Handel's *Acis and Galatea* and replaced the organ
with wind instruments. He also made changes to
Handel's *Messiah*, turning some of the arias into
recitatives. Van Swieten was pleased, but the work
was unworthy of Mozart's genius and did not even
bring in much money.

   In 1789 Constanze became pregnant for the
fifth time, and the household's finances were in as
parlous a state as ever. A chance seemed to present
itself in April, however, when a former pupil,
Prince Karl Lichnowsky, left for Berlin and invited
Mozart to accompany him. On the way they passed
through Prague and Dresden, where Mozart
performed both at court and at the residence of
the Russian ambassador (who found him "very
learned, very difficult, and consequently very
esteemed by instrumentalists"), and through
Leipzig, where he played Johann Sebastian Bach's
organ in St. Thomas's Church.

   On 25 April the travelers were at the court of

After Mozart's
death, Constanze
dedicated the score
of one of his piano
concertos (above) to the
music-loving Prince
Ludwig Ferdinand of
Prussia (1772–1806).

Frederick William II of Prussia, in Berlin. Frederick William, like his late uncle Frederick the Great, was a music lover. He later maintained that Mozart refused his offer of the post of Kapellmeister. Whatever the truth of this assertion, he certainly welcomed the composer cordially and commissioned string quartets and piano sonatas for his daughter Frederike.
But Mozart stayed only seven days.
Following Lichnowsky, he left on 2 May, stopping again in Leipzig to give a

Only two of the six children born to Wolfgang and Constanze survived infancy. Karl Thomas (below right) went into administration, and Franz Xaver Wolfgang became a composer, signing his works "Wolfgang Amadeus Mozart." Both remained bachelors and died childless. This portrait dates from 1798.

Der Thomas kirch hof in Leipzig

recital there on the 12th. He quarreled with the prince, however, and—contrary to plans and economic prudence—returned to Berlin, where he appeared before the queen.

The church in Leipzig where the elder Bach had led the choir.

Mozart Returned Home After a Two-Month Absence, Poorer Than Ever

Constanze was suffering from an infected foot and had to go to the spa at Baden for treatment. This was a heavy expense, and Mozart again was forced to ask for loans: "I beg and implore you, in God's name, for whatever temporary help you can give me" (letter to Puchberg, 17 July 1789).

A revival of *The Marriage of Figaro* in August brought a note of relief, for it led to a commission for a new opera from the emperor. Joseph II himself chose the subject, *Così Fan Tutte, Ossia la Scuola Degli Amanti* ("Women are all the same, or the school for lovers"), inspired by an anecdote that was making the rounds of the salons. Da Ponte once again wrote the libretto.

The pair had to work fast—the premiere was planned for January 1790. Mozart's friends followed

Frederick William II of Prussia, cellist and lover of chamber music.

its progress with affectionate concern, as the last months of the year were clouded by tragedy: Another baby, Anna Maria, born on 16 November, had lived only an hour. Yet somehow Mozart found time to respond to a request for a composition from a fellow Mason, the clarinetist Anton Stadler, with the Clarinet Quintet K. 581. The voice of Mozart's favorite instrument soars with gorgeous lyricism in this work, which heralded the masterpieces of his two final years.

Despite Plots Believed to Have Been Engineered by Salieri, *Così Fan Tutte* Was Produced

The new opera was performed on 26 January 1790. Its favorable reception was mingled with incomprehension: The subject was considered

The opera *Così Fan Tutte* is Mozart's most complex exploration of truth, falsehood, fidelity, and betrayal. In this silhouette by Lotte Reiniger, one of the heroes, disguised as an Albanian, woos his friend's fiancée.

Introduzzione

The silhouette below typifies the fun-loving Dorabella as she sings of Cupid's pranks in her Act II aria, "E amore un ladroncello" ("Love is a little thief").

amusing, the subtle cruelty not fully appreciated. The opera's success was clouded by another calamity, the death of the emperor. Joseph II had been a reliable protector if not a generous one; Leopold II, while retaining Mozart's services, paid little attention to him— just at a time when Mozart so sorely needed aid. For, perhaps overburdened by financial worries, Mozart's own health had begun to suffer. He wrote little during 1790, indeed nothing between January and May, when he finished the last two quartets in the set dedicated to the king of Prussia.

Mozart applied for the post of assistant Kapellmeister but was turned down. The new sovereign's lack of interest in him was proved conclusively when, unlike his colleagues, Mozart was not invited either to the celebrations in honor of Ferdinand and Maria Carolina of Naples or to Leopold's coronation in Frankfurt on 9 October. Mozart went at his own expense, pawning silver and furniture to pay his way.

Part of the score of *Così* (top), and a playbill for its premiere (above). The conflict between desire and commitment at the heart of the opera was not fully understood at this time, and in the 19th century the music was even given a different set of words. Yet to modern audiences, the fundamental ambiguity of *Così* constitutes its greatest appeal.

The Last Months: Misery and Divine Inspiration

Hardly had he returned to Vienna from Frankfurt than a new opportunity arose: Mozart was asked to write two operas for London. But he would have to spend six months in the English capital, and how was he to do this with no money? He was forced to refuse, and with tears in his eyes watched Joseph Haydn set off in his stead. He pulled himself together and began to compose again and to look for pupils. He wrote the String Quintet K. 593 and then the Piano Concerto no. 27 (K. 595). Far from betraying his suffering, these works seem to contain a new verve and popular appeal. In March came some good news: Emanuel Schikaneder, who had taken over as director of Vienna's Theater auf der Wieden in 1789, gave him the libretto for *The Magic Flute*, which Mozart accepted with alacrity.

Meanwhile, Constanze had returned to Baden. Concerned about her health, Mozart joined her for a few days in June; but apart from that, he stayed in Vienna and worked.

Now Seriously Ill, Mozart Threw the Last of His Energy into Two Operas

Schikaneder, a fellow Freemason, kept an eye on Mozart and even lent him a house near the theater, where he could compose and relax with a circle of friends. On 26 July 1791 Mozart's sixth child (though so far only one, Karl, had survived), Franz Xaver Wolfgang, was born.

It was at about this time that Mozart received from an unknown man an

A playbill announcing the premiere of *The Magic Flute*. Fairy tale, philosophical fable, Masonic opera—it was all these and more.

Papageno, a bird catcher, in a 1791 engraving (left), and two scenes from *The Magic Flute* (opposite): Papageno charms the animals, and the high priest Sarastro appears.

The model for the wise Sarastro was probably Count Ignaz von Born, Freemason and eminent mineralogist, who had come to Vienna at the request of Maria Theresa. Mozart wrote the cantata *The Masons' Joy* in his honor.

Genesis of a Masterpiece

Mozart had not expected to have another opportunity to write a German opera, but Emanuel Schikaneder suggested to him the idea of *The Magic Flute*. The several sources for the plot include *Sethos,* a novel set in ancient Egypt by Jean Terrasson, Paul Wranitzky's opera *Oberon, King of the Elves,* and Liebeskind's fairy tale "Lulu, or the Magic Flute." Schikaneder wrote most of the libretto and also sang Papageno in the premiere. This set design for the palace of the Queen of the Night was designed by noted German architect Karl Friedrich Schinkel for a Berlin production in 1816. Below: A 19th-century Sarastro.

The Stuff of Heroes

The plot of *The Magic Flute* centers on three couples: The young hero Tamino is willing to endure the trials of initiation at the side of his beloved Pamina; Papageno, the bird catcher, may be seen as Tamino's counterpart— for all his enduring naïveté and childlike common sense, he is ready to die if he cannot find his sweetheart, Papagena; and the wise Sarastro, symbolizing light and goodness, confronts and finally overcomes the power of darkness represented by the Queen of the Night. Left: Schinkel's set for Sarastro's garden. Below: Monostatos, Sarastro's Moorish servant.

The Influence of Freemasonry

On one level *The Magic Flute* seems like an oriental fairy tale, with its monsters, genies, and metamorphoses, but it also reflects the Masonic interests of both composer and librettist. These are evident in the initiation rituals that the chief protagonists must undergo, the allusions to ancient Egypt, and the iconography of numbers. But the opera's message of love, brotherhood, and sublime wisdom transcends such specific details. Left: The Queen of the Night, as conceived by Simon Quaglio for a Munich production in 1818. Below: The same character in another 19th-century production.

unsigned letter containing a commission for a requiem mass. (This odd event has become the subject of endless speculation, but is in fact easily explained: A certain Count Franz von Walsegg, who fancied himself a composer, wanted a requiem for his late wife, to be passed off as his own work. The mysterious stranger who delivered the order was his servant.) Mozart was exhausted; he had yet to complete *The Magic Flute,* and he had received a new commission from the national theater in Prague for an opera to celebrate the coronation of Leopold II as King of Bohemia on 6 September. Yet he agreed to write the requiem for this stranger.

The composition of *La Clemenza di Tito* (*The Clemency of Titus*), his last Italian opera, took just eighteen days from start to finish. He worked at it constantly, even during the journey to Prague for the coronation. He was delighted to be back in this city, which he liked so much and where he felt appreciated. He returned to Vienna in mid-September, completely worn out.

Despite his poor health and spirits, Mozart wanted to finish *The Magic Flute* in time for its premiere on 30 September, and he did. It was a triumph. The theater was packed, and the audience, which this time consisted of townspeople rather than the ladies and gentlemen of the salons, gave it a huge ovation. *The Magic Flute* was Mozart's last opera.

The Requiem

Mozart was exhausted. He used his remaining strength to compose the Clarinet Concerto K. 622 and to start the *Requiem.* In these efforts he was helped by a pupil, Franz Xaver Süssmayer. Together they worked desperately. By the end of November Mozart's illness had him in its grip: His hands and feet were swollen and partly paralyzed. He made one last attempt to finish the *Requiem,* but the manuscript breaks off after only a few bars of the *Lacrymosa* movement.

" His last movement was an attempt to express with his mouth a drum passage in the *Requiem.* I can hear it still. "
Sophie Haibel
(Mozart's sister-in-law)
1825

M*ozart Composing the Requiem,* a painting by W. D. Grant.

On 4 December his condition deteriorated further, and he knew he was about to die. Priests were summoned, but they hesitated to come to the deathbed of a Freemason. Mozart remained calm. Late that evening he fell into a coma. The end came just before one o'clock in the morning.

His funeral was quite modest. A few devoted friends followed the simple procession, but Constanze was too ill to attend. The body was placed in a communal grave without even a cross. Such was the tragic end of the life that had begun with seemingly limitless promise.

"I have come to the end before having enjoyed my talent. Life was so lovely, my career opened under such happy auspices, but one cannot change one's destiny. No one can know the measure of his days; one must resign oneself, for it will all go as Providence decrees. I end my days; here is my requiem which I must not leave unfinished."

Mozart
September 1791

DOCUMENTS

Fascinating family correspondence, candid
portraits sketched by contemporaries, and
varied assessments by composers, critics, and
performers all attest to the extraordinary
nature of Mozart's genius and his life.

Correspondence

Mozart's letters tell frankly of his joys and troubles, frustrations and struggles. Like his compositions, they are full of sensitivity and tenderness. These examples are taken from Mozart: Briefe und Aufzeichnungen *(Mozart: Letters and Notes), a 1962 edition of Mozart's correspondence.*

In Milan, having just finished composing his opera Lucio Silla, *Mozart relaxes by writing to his sister. He writes in a characteristically comic vein.*

[Milan, 18 December 1772]

To Nannerl

I hope you are well, my dear sister. When you receive this letter, my dear sister, my opera will be being performed that same evening. Think of me, my dear sister, and do your best to imagine, my dear sister, that you are watching and hearing it too, my dear sister. Admittedly that is difficult, as it is already eleven o'clock; what's more, I believe beyond any doubt that during the day it is brighter than at Easter. My dear sister, tomorrow we dine at Herr von Mayer's, and why is this, do you think? Guess! Because he has invited us. Tomorrow's rehearsal is at the theater, but the impresario, Signor Castiglioni, has urged me not to say anything about it, because otherwise everybody will come rushing along, and we don't want that. So, my child, I beg you not to tell anyone anything about it. Otherwise too many people would come rushing along. That reminds me, do you know what happened here today? I'll tell you. We left Count Firmian's to go home and when we reached our street, we opened the front door and what do you suppose happened then? We went in. Goodbye, my little lung. I embrace you, my liver, and remain, my stomach, ever your unworthy brother

Wolfgang

Please, my dear sister, something is biting me—please scratch me.

Leopold and Wolfgang Mozart.

Hannibal Platz (now Makart Platz), Salzburg, lies across the river from the cathedral and castle. The Mozarts moved into the house on the right in 1773, and Leopold lived there until his death in 1787. In the background are the domed church of the Holy Trinity and a hill crowned by the Capuchin monastery.

This petition from Wolfgang to Count Hieronymus Colloredo, archbishop of Salzburg, was actually written by Leopold and signed by his son. A penciled note in the archbishop's hand reads: "To the Court Chamberlain with my decision that father and son have my firm permission to seek their fortune elsewhere."

1 August 1777

Your Grace, most worthy Prince of the Holy Roman Empire!

I will not presume to trouble Your Grace with a detailed description of our unhappy circumstances, of which my father respectfully gave an exact account in his humble petition which was handed to you on 14 March 1777. As, however, your hoped-for consent

was not forthcoming, my father intended last June most respectfully to beg Your Grace once more to allow us to travel for a few months in order to recover our fortunes somewhat; and he would have done so, if Your Grace had not given orders that in view of the pending visit of His Majesty the Emperor your orchestra should hold itself in readiness for all contingencies.

Later my father again respectfully requested a leave of absence, but Your Grace refused it, your gracious decision being that I, who am in any case only half in your service, could travel alone. Our situation is pressing; my father therefore decided to let me go on my own. But even so Your Grace has been pleased to raise certain objections. Most gracious Prince and Lord! Parents endeavor to endow their children with the ability to earn their own bread, and they should do this in their own interest and that of the State. The greater the talents that children have received from God, the more they ought to use them to improve their own circumstances and those of their parents, to stand by their parents and to work toward their own advancement and a secure future.

The Gospel instructs us on this proper use of talents. My conscience tells me that I owe it to God to be grateful to my father, who has spent his time tirelessly on my education, so that I may lighten his burden and provide for myself and later on for my sister. For I should be sorry to think that she had spent so many hours at the harpsichord and was still unable to make the best use of her training.

Your Grace will therefore be so good as to allow me to ask you most humbly for a leave of absence, which I should like to take at the beginning of autumn, so that I am not exposed to the inclement weather of the coming winter months. Your Grace will not receive this petition ungraciously, for when I asked you for permission to travel to Vienna three years ago, you graciously declared that I had nothing to hope for in Salzburg and would do better to seek my fortune elsewhere.

I thank your Grace most respectfully for all the favors I have received from you, and, with the earnest hope of being able to serve you in my mature years with greater success,

I remain your most humble
and obedient servant
Wolfgang Amadé Mozart

Mozart complains to his father about Paris and its citizens.

Paris, 31 July 1778

Monsieur mon très cher père!

…M. Grimm said to me the other day: "What am I to tell your father? What course do you intend to pursue? Are you staying here or going to Mannheim?" I really could not help laughing. "What am I supposed to do in Mannheim now?" I said, "I wish I had never come to Paris—but so it is. I am here and I must use every effort to make a success of it." "Well," he said, "I hardly think that you will achieve much in Paris." "Why not?" I asked. "I see a crowd of second-rate bunglers getting on fine; why shouldn't I, with my talents?"… "Well," he said, "I am afraid that you are not being sufficiently active here—you do not get about enough."…

What annoys me most of all is that these stupid French people seem to think I am still seven years old, because that was my age when they first saw me. They treat me as a beginner—except of course the real musicians, who think differently. But it is the majority that counts.

I shall do my utmost to get along here by teaching and to earn as much money as possible, which I am now doing in the fond hope that my circumstances may soon change; for I cannot deny, and must confess, that I should be delighted to be released from this place. Giving lessons here is no joke. It is exhausting; unless you take a large number of pupils, you cannot make much money. You must not think that this is laziness on my part—not at all. It just goes completely against my genius and the way I live. You know that I have

A silk writing case that belonged to Mozart.

my being, so to speak, entirely in music, I am immersed in it all day long and love to try out ideas, work on them, and mull them over. Well, I am prevented from doing this by my way of life here. True, I shall have a few hours free, but I shall need those few hours more for rest than for work. I told you in my last letter about the opera. I cannot help it—I must write a full-scale opera or none at all. If I write a small one, I shall get very little for it (for everything is taxed here). And should it have the misfortune not to please these stupid French, all would be over—I would never get the chance to compose another—I would have gained nothing by it—and my reputation would have suffered. If, on the other hand, I write a full-length opera, the remuneration will be better—I shall be doing the work

I like best and am best at—and I shall have better hopes of success, for with a large-scale work you have a better chance of making your name. I assure you that if I am commissioned to write an opera, I shall have no qualms at all. True, this language [i.e., French] is an invention of the devil—and I fully realize the difficulties which all composers have encountered. But in spite of this I feel I am just as capable of overcoming them as anyone else. On the contrary, whenever I fancy, as I often do, that I have got the commission, my whole body seems to be on fire, and I tremble from head to foot with eagerness to teach the French more thoroughly to know, appreciate, and fear the Germans. For why is a full-length opera never entrusted to a Frenchman? Why must it always be a foreigner? For me the most detestable aspect would be the singers. Well, I am ready—I wish to avoid quarrels—but if I am challenged, I shall know how to defend myself. But I should prefer to avoid a duel, for I do not care to wrestle with dwarfs.

Wolfgang Amadé Mozart

As time went on, a rupture with the archbishop of Salzburg became inevitable. Mozart longed for it and, desperate for liberty, finally provoked it. He reports to his father:

Vienna, 9 May 1781

Mon très cher père!

I am still seething with rage! And I am sure that you, my dearest and most beloved father, are equally angry with me. My patience has been tried for so long that at last it has given out. I am no longer so unfortunate as to be in Salzburg's service. Today is a happy day for me. I'll tell you what happened.

Twice already that—I don't know what to call him—has said to my face the greatest *sottises* [insults] and *impertinences*, which I did not repeat to you, out of consideration for your feelings, and for which I only refrained from taking my revenge at the time because you, my dear father, were ever before my eyes. He called me a lout and a dissolute wretch and told me to be off. And I—endured it all, although I felt that not only my honor but yours too was being attacked. But, in accordance with your wish, I remained silent. Now read this.

A week ago a footman came up unexpectedly and told me to clear out that very instant. All the others had been informed of the day of their departure, all but me. So I hastily threw everything into my trunk, and old

The square known as the Graben, at the heart of Vienna. The city was ideal for a composer: The Viennese loved celebrations, and music was an important part of daily life.

Madame Weber has been good enough to take me into her house. I have a lovely room, and I am living with people who are obliging and who supply me with all the things which one often requires in a hurry and which one does not have when living alone....

one served him as badly as I did—he advised me to leave today or else he would write home and have my salary stopped. I couldn't get a word in edgeways, for he raged on like a fire. I listened to it all without losing control. He lied to my face that my salary was five hundred gulden, called me a scoundrel, an oaf, a good-for-nothing. Oh, I really do not wish to tell you all he said. At last my blood began to boil and I said, "So Your Grace is not satisfied with me?" "What, are you threatening me—you scoundrel? There is the door! I want nothing more to do with you, you wretched youth." At last I said: "Nor I with you!" "Well, get out then!" On my way out, I said, "This is final. You shall have it tomorrow in writing."

Tell me now, my dear father, did I not speak out too late rather than too soon? The point is, my honor means more to me than anything else, and I know that you feel the same. Do not worry about me at all. I am so sure of my success here [in Vienna] that I would have left even without the slightest reason; and since I now have a very good reason to do so—in fact three reasons—I have nothing to gain by delaying any longer. On the contrary—I had played the coward twice, and I just could not do so a third time.

As long as the Archbishop remains here, I shall not give a concert. You seem convinced that I am putting myself in a bad light with the Emperor and the nobility, but that is quite wrong; the Archbishop is hated here, and by the Emperor most of all.... By the next post I shall send you a little money to show you that I am not starving. Now please be cheerful, for my happiness is just beginning, and I

When I presented myself today, the valets informed me that the Archbishop wanted to give me a parcel to take charge of. I asked whether it was urgent. They told me, "Yes, it is of the greatest importance."... When I went in to the Archbishop...his first words were: *Archbishop*: "Well, boy, when are you leaving?" *I*: "I intended to go tonight, but all the seats were already taken." That started him off—I was the most despicable wretch he knew—no trust that my happiness will be yours also. Write to me in cypher that you are pleased—and indeed you really can be pleased—but in public find fault with me as much as you like, so that no blame falls on you....

I want nothing more to do with Salzburg. I hate the Archbishop to distraction.

Adieu. I kiss your hands a thousand times and embrace my dear sister with all my heart and am ever your obedient son.

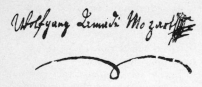

In this letter to his father, Mozart explains his conception of the relationship of words to music in opera.

Vienna
13 October 1781

Mon très cher père!

...It is my view that in an opera the poetry must be without question the obedient daughter of the music. Why are Italian comic operas so popular everywhere—in spite of their miserable libretti—even in Paris, where I myself witnessed their success? Because the music is all-important, and when one listens to it one forgets everything else. An opera is all the more sure of success when the plot is well worked out and the words are written solely for the music and not added here and there for the sake of some silly rhyme, which, God knows, contributes

nothing to the value of any theatrical performance, whatever it is, but rather detracts from it—I mean, words or even entire verses that ruin the composer's whole concept. Verse is indeed the most indispensable element for music—but rhymes for their own sake are the most detrimental. Those pretentious people who set to work in this pedantic fashion will always come to grief, and so will their music. The best thing of all is when a good composer, who understands the stage and is talented enough to have ideas of his own, comes across a skillful poet, that true phoenix; then one need have no worries even concerning the applause of the ignorant. Librettists seem to me almost like trumpeters with their tricks of the trade! If we composers were always to stick just as faithfully to our rules (which were good enough at a time when no one knew better), we would be producing music just as mediocre as their mediocre libretti.

Well, I think I have chattered enough nonsense to you; so I must now enquire about what is dearest of all to me: your health, my dearest father!...

I trust that my sister is improving daily. I kiss her with all my heart and, my dearest, most beloved father, I kiss your hands a thousand times and am ever your most obedient son

W. A. Mozart

Mozart writes to his father to inform him of his decision to marry Constanze Weber.

Vienna, 15 December 1781

Dearest father,

You demand an explanation of the words at the end of my last letter. How gladly I would have opened my heart to you long ago, but I was discouraged from doing so by the reproach which I knew you might have made me for *thinking about such a thing at an inappropriate time*— although to think can never be inappropriate.

My efforts in the meantime are directed to acquiring a small but *steady* income here, for then one can live quite well with the help of the irregular extra sums; and then I intend—to marry! Are you appalled at the idea? But, dear, kind father, please read on. I have had to reveal to you what is on my mind; now allow me to reveal my reasons too.

The voice of nature speaks just as loudly in me as in anyone else, perhaps louder than in many a big strong lout. It is impossible for me to live as most young men do today; in the first place, I am too deeply religious, secondly I am too compassionate and too honorable to wish to lead some innocent girl astray, and thirdly I have too much horror and revulsion, fear and apprehension of disease, and solicitude for my health, to romp about with whores, and I can swear to never having done such a thing....

I know that this reason, strong though it is, is not sufficient in itself. But my temperament, which is more inclined toward a peaceful domestic existence than to riotous living—I who from my childhood have never been accustomed to look after my own things—clothes, linen, and so on— can think of nothing I need more than a wife.

I assure you that I often spend more money than necessary because I do not pay heed to those things—I am quite convinced that with a wife, and the same income that I have as a single man, I would manage better. How much needless expenditure would then be avoided?—true, one then has other expenses, but one knows what they are and can allow for them—in short, one can lead a well-regulated life. A bachelor, to my mind, lives only half a life. That is my mind and I cannot change it....

So who, then, is the object of my love? Once again, please do not be appalled—surely not one of the Webers? Yes, one of the Webers— not Josepha, not Sophie, but Costanza [*sic*], the middle one.... My dear, good Constanze is the martyr of the family, and is, perhaps for that very reason, the kindest, most capable, in short the best of them all....

She is not ugly but not at all beautiful. Her beauty consists entirely in two little dark eyes and a lovely figure. She is not witty, but she has enough common sense to be able to fulfill her duties as a wife and mother. She is not inclined to be extravagant; it would be quite wrong to say she was. On the contrary, she is used to being poorly clad, for whatever their mother had to spare was always given to the others, never to her. She would like to be nicely, neatly dressed, but does not aspire to elegance. Most of what a young lady requires she can do for herself, and she always dresses her own hair.

She understands household economy and has the kindest heart in the world—I love her, and she genuinely loves me. Tell me, could I wish for a better wife?...

I kiss your hands a thousand times and am ever your obedient son

W. A. Mozart

The Theresienbaden, a bathing establishment in the spa town of Baden near Vienna, seen in Mozart's time.

In the late 1780s, Mozart's condition—both physical and financial—went from bad to worse. He wrote numerous letters urgently requesting money from fellow Mason Johann Michael Puchberg, who appears to have been the only person he could turn to.

Vienna, 17 May 1790

Dearest friend and brother Mason,

...I am at the moment so devoid of funds that I must beg you, dearest friend, in God's name, to support me with however much you can spare. If, as I hope, I get the other money in a week or two, I will immediately repay what you lend me now—as to what I have owed you for so long already, I must ask you to continue to be patient. If you only knew what grief and worry all this causes me....

Next Saturday I intend to perform my quartets at my home, and you and your wife are most cordially invited. Dearest, best friend and brother, please do not withdraw your friendship on account of my importunity, but stand by me. I rely wholly on you and remain ever yours in deepest gratitude,

Mozart

I have two pupils at present and should like to increase the number to eight—please spread the word that I am willing to give lessons.

In 1791 Constanze became ill and had to go to the spa at Baden for a cure. Mozart, full of solicitude, wrote to her every day.

Vienna
Wednesday, 6 July 1791

Dearest, most beloved little wife,

I received with indescribable pleasure the news that you had received the money safely. I cannot remember writing to you that you should settle *all* the bills! How could I, a rational creature, have written that? But so it is—I must have done it without thinking, which is quite possible, as I have so many important things on my mind just now. My intention was *only* that you should pay for your *baths*—the rest was for your own use, and as for the remaining expenses, which I have already reckoned up, I will deal with them when I arrive.... Our life is not exactly very enjoyable. But let's be patient—I'm sure things will improve, and then I shall rest in your arms!

At the moment you can give me no greater pleasure than by being cheerful and content—for if I know for sure that *you have all you need,* then all my efforts are a pleasure to be welcomed; the direst, most difficult situation I might find myself in would present no problem if I know that you are *in good health and spirits.* Farewell...think of me and talk of me often—love me forever as I love you, and be ever my Stanzi Marini, as I shall ever be your
Stu!—Knaller paller—
schnip—schnap—schnur—
Schnepeperl.
snai!—

Give X. a box on the ears and tell him you were trying to swat a fly that I had spied on his face! Farewell. Watch now—catch—x x x—three kisses, sweet as sugar, are flying toward you!

Mozart writes again to Constanze at Baden. In this letter, as in the previous one, "X." represents a name crossed out in the letter by a later hand.

Vienna
7 July 1791

Dearest, most beloved little wife!

You will forgive me, I know, for only sending you one letter a day. The reason is that I must keep track of X. and not let him escape. I am at his house every day at seven o'clock in the morning.

I hope you got the letter I wrote you yesterday.... My one wish now is to get my affairs settled so that I can be with you again. You cannot imagine how dreadfully I have been missing you all this time. I can't describe what I have been feeling—a kind of emptiness which is really painful—a kind of longing, which is never satisfied and never ceases, which persists and indeed increases day by day. When I think what fun we had together at Baden, like a pair of children, and what sad, weary hours I am spending here! Even my work gives me no pleasure, because I am accustomed to break off from working now and then and exchange a few words with you—a pleasure which, sadly, is not possible now. If I go to the piano and sing something out of my opera [*The Magic Flute*], I have to stop at once, as I get overcome by emotion. *Basta!* The very hour after I finish this business I shall be up and away from here.

I have no news to tell you....
Adieu, dearest little wife.
Ever your
Mozart

Mozart Through the Eyes of His Contemporaries

Many vivid accounts of Mozart survive in portraits written by relatives, friends, and comparative strangers. All share a sense of wonder at encountering the inexplicable phenomenon of genius.

As a child, Mozart's sister Maria Anna ("Nannerl") played the keyboard as brilliantly as her brother, but after she turned sixteen, Leopold left her behind when he took Wolfgang abroad. Because she was a woman, there was no thought of a career for her as a professional musician. She tried her hand at composing and was enthusiastically encouraged by Wolfgang, but her efforts were ignored by her father. After Wolfgang's marriage, brother and sister seem rarely to have met or corresponded, perhaps partly because Maria Anna shared her father's disapproval of Constanze. In 1792, after Wolfgang's death, Maria Anna provided information about him for his publishers at their request. Her accounts exhibit a cool, studied objectivity.

Wolfgang was small, thin, pale, and totally unremarkable in both face and figure. Except in music, he was and remained more or less a child, and this is a dominant feature of the negative side of his character. He would always have needed a father, mother, or other mentor; he could not manage money; and he married, against his father's wishes, a girl who was quite unsuitable for him—hence the great disorder in the household at the time of his death and afterward.

From childhood on he used to play and compose at nighttime and in the early morning. If he sat down at the keyboard at nine o'clock, it was impossible to get him away from it before midnight. I believe he would have played all night. Between six and nine in the morning he generally

Leopold, Wolfgang, and Nannerl performing in Paris in 1763.

composed in bed, then he got up and composed nothing throughout the day unless a composition was required in a great hurry.... I do not remember him ever practicing after the age of seven, for his practice consisted in playing to other people: He liked pieces to be put before him which he would then sight-read. That was how he practiced.

Letter to Friedrich Schlichtegroll
from Maria Anna Mozart,
Mozart: Briefe und Aufzeichnungen,
vol. IV, 1962

In a letter written on 24 April 1794 to Maria Anna Mozart, Andreas Schachtner, court trumpeter at Salzburg and a close friend of the family, recalls memories of Mozart as a little boy of seven.

You ask what your late brother's favorite pastimes were when he was a child, when he was not making music. No reply is possible to this question; for as soon as he had become devoted to music, all his senses were as if dead to all else, and even the usual childish games and amusements had to be accompanied by music if they were to hold his attention; if he and I ever took toys or games from one room to another, whichever of us was empty-handed had to sing a march or play one on the violin....

You will remember that I possess a very good violin that little Wolfgangerl always used to call the butter violin because of its soft, mellow tone. Once, soon after your return from Vienna, he had a go on it and could not find words enough to praise it. A day or two later I came to visit him again and found him about to start amusing himself on his own violin. He immediately said, "How is your butter violin today?" and carried on extemporizing on his own. After a while he became thoughtful and said, "Herr Schachtner, your violin is tuned half a quarter-tone lower than mine; if only you would get it tuned...." I laughed, but his father, who knew the boy's extraordinary aural memory and sense of pitch, asked me to fetch my violin to see if he was right. I did so, and he was indeed right....

Just after your return from Vienna [in 1763], from where Wolfgang had brought back a little violin he had been given, the late Herr Wenzl brought by six trios that he had written during your father's absence. Herr Wenzl was one of the outstanding violinists of the time who was just starting off as a composer, and he wanted your father's opinion. We played these trios, with your father playing the bass part on his viola, Herr Wenzl playing first violin, and myself second. Little Wolfgangerl asked if he could play second violin, but his father dismissed his request as ridiculous, for the boy had no idea about violin playing, and his father thought he would be quite incapable of it. Wolfgang said: "You don't need to have learned if you're playing second." His father ordered him to leave the room and stop disturbing us. Wolfgang burst out sobbing and moved toward the door carrying his violin, dragging his feet. I asked for him to be allowed to play along with me. At length his father said, "Play with Herr Schachtner, but very quietly so that no one can hear you—otherwise, out you go!" So Wolfgang played with me. Soon I realized with astonishment that I was quite superfluous. I laid down my violin and looked at your father. While this was going on, tears of admiration and dawning expectation were running down his cheeks. And so Wolfgang played all the trios. When we had come to the end, Wolfgang was sufficiently emboldened by our admiration to assert that he could even play first violin. We tried this out just for fun, and were convulsed with mirth, for though he played it with utterly wrong, haphazard technique, he never quite had to give up.

Finally, a word about the acuteness and sensitivity of his ear. Until he was nearly ten he had an uncontrollable terror of the trumpet when played alone, without other instruments; if anyone so much as showed him a trumpet it was like holding a loaded pistol to his heart. His father wished to rid him of this childish fear and ordered me to blow a trumpet at him regardless of his entreaties, but, my goodness, I wish I had not allowed myself to be persuaded to do so, for hardly had little Wolfgangerl heard the first blaring note than he turned pale and began to fall to the floor; if I had continued, he would certainly have gone into convulsions.

Letter to Maria Anna Mozart
from Andreas Schachtner,
Mozart: Briefe und Aufzeichnungen,
vol. IV, 1962

The same astonishment at Mozart's precociousness is found in the Literary Correspondence *of Baron Grimm, Mozart's patron and sincere admirer in Paris.*

1 December 1763

Real prodigies are so rare that when they do appear, everyone talks about them. A [vice] Kapellmeister from Salzburg called Mozart has just arrived here with two delightful-looking children. His daughter, aged eleven, plays the harpsichord quite brilliantly; she executes the longest, most difficult pieces with astounding precision. Her brother, who will be seven in January, is a phenomenon so extraordinary that one can scarcely believe one's eyes and ears. This child thinks nothing of performing the most difficult pieces with perfect accuracy with hands that can hardly stretch a sixth. What is quite incredible is to see him playing extempore for an hour at a time, abandoning himself to his own inspiration and to a wealth of ravishing ideas, which he has no trouble in stringing together with taste and clarity. . . .

He thinks nothing of deciphering anything you put before him: He writes and composes with marvelous facility, without needing to go to the harpsichord to find the chords. . . . You will guess that he has no difficulty in playing any piece you give him in a different key and in any time signature you specify; but I have seen something else no less incredible. The other day, a lady asked him if he would accompany her by ear, without seeing the music, in an Italian cavatina that she knew by heart, and she began to sing. The child tried out a bass which was not absolutely right, because it is impossible to prepare the accompaniment of a song that one does not know; but when the song was over, he asked her to sing it again, and this time he not only played the melody with the right hand but added the bass with the left without hesitation. After this he asked her to sing it ten more times and changed the style of his accompaniment each time;

N o. 180 Ebury Street, where the Mozart family stayed during their 1764 visit to London.

Daines Barrington (1727–1800), an English lawyer and antiquarian, writing to the secretary of the Royal Society (a scientific organization founded in London in 1662), gives the following account of the boy Mozart, having seen him in London in June 1765.

Sir,

If I was to send you a well-attested account of a boy who measured seven feet in height, when he was not more than eight years of age, it might be considered as not undeserving the notice of the Royal Society.

The instance which I now desire you will communicate to that learned body, of as early an exertion of most extraordinary musical talents, seems perhaps equally to claim their attention.…

Having been informed … that he was often visited with musical ideas, to which, even in the midst of the night, he would give utterance on his harpsichord; I told his father that I should be glad to hear some of his extemporary flights.

The father shook his head at this, saying, that it depended entirely upon his being as it were musically inspired, but that I might ask him whether he was in humour for such a composition.

Happening to know that little Mozart was much taken notice of by Manzoli, the famous singer, who came over to England in 1764, I said to the boy, that I should be glad to hear an extempore *Love Song,* such as his friend Manzoli might choose in an opera.

The boy on this (who continued to sit at his harpsichord) looked back with much archness and immediately began five or six lines of a jargon recitative proper to introduce a love song. He

he would have done it twenty times if he had not been asked to stop.…

Monsieur Mozart's children have earned the admiration of everyone who has seen them. The Emperor and Empress overwhelmed them with kindness, and they were given the same reception at the courts of Munich and Mannheim. It is a pity that people are so ignorant on musical matters here in France. The father intends to proceed to England and to bring his children back via southern Germany.

Friedrich Melchior von Grimm,
*Correspondance Littéraire,
Philosophique et Critique,* 1763

played a symphony which might correspond with an air composed to the single word, *Affetto*. It had a first and second part, which, together with the symphonies, was of the length that opera songs generally last: if this extemporary composition was not amazingly capital, yet it was really above mediocrity, and shewed most extraordinary readiness of invention. Finding that he was in humour, and as it were inspired, I then desired him to compose a *Song of Rage*, such as might be proper to the opera stage. The boy again looked back with much archness, and began five or six lines of a jargon recitative proper to precede a *Song of Anger*. This lasted also about the same time with the *Song of Love*; and in the middle of it he had worked himself up to such a pitch, that he beat his harpsichord like a person possessed, rising sometimes in his chair. The word he pitched upon for this second extemporary composition was *Perfido*. After this he played a difficult lesson, which he had finished a day or two before; his execution was amazing, considering that his little fingers could scarcely reach a sixth on the harpsichord.

His astonishing readiness, however, did not arise merely from great practice; he had a thorough knowledge of the fundamental principles of composition, as, upon producing a treble, he immediately wrote a bass under it, which, when tried, had a very good effect.

He was also a great master of modulation, and his transitions from one key to another were excessively natural and judicious; he practised in this manner for a considerable time with a handkerchief over the keys of the harpsichord.

The facts which I have been mentioning, I was myself an eye-witness of; to which I must add, that I have been informed by two or three able musicians, when [Johann Christian] Bach the celebrated composer had begun a fugue and left off abruptly, that little Mozart hath immediately taken it up, and worked it after a most masterly manner.

Witness as I was myself of most of these extraordinary facts, I must own that I could not help suspecting his father imposed with regard to the real age of the boy, though he had not only a most childish appearance, but likewise had all the actions of that stage of life. For example, whilst he was playing to me, a favourite cat came in, upon which he immediately left his harpsichord, nor could we bring him back for a considerable time. He would also sometimes run about the room with a stick between his legs by way of horse....

Daines Barrington,
in *The Philosophical Transactions*
(the Royal Society's journal),
vol. LX, 1770

This description of Mozart by his sister-in-law Sophie Haibel (1763–1846) is recorded in the first biography of him, written by Georg Nikolaus Nissen, Constanze Mozart's second husband.

He was always good-humored, but even in the best of moods he was still pensive. He would look you keenly in the eye and give a thoughtful answer to anything you said, whether serious or lighthearted, yet he always seemed to be deeply preoccupied with something quite different. Even while washing his hands in the morning, he would be pacing restlessly up and down the room, his mind working hard. At the dining table he would often take a corner of his napkin, screw it up tightly and rub it around under his nose without seeming to be aware what he was doing.… In his lighter moments he was keenly interested in each new pastime, for instance, riding or billiards.… His hands and feet were in constant motion; he was always fingering something or other—his hat, pockets, watch-chain, tables, chairs—as if he were playing on a keyboard.

The next three passages are also taken from Nissen's biography.

His hearing was so highly developed and he could discern differences in pitch with such perfect accuracy that he could detect minute flaws in intonation even in the largest orchestra and could identify which player or instrument was the culprit. Then this man, normally so gentle and good-humored, would fly into a passion and express himself with the utmost vehemence.

It is known that he once got up from the piano in the middle of a recital and walked out on his audience because they were not paying attention. He was often criticized for doing this; but unjustly so. Everything he played he felt to the depth of his being: He was all emotion and concentration. How then could he remain in this state if faced with cool indifference or inattention, let alone intrusive chatting?

Throughout his life it was frequently said of him—more as an ignorant form of praise than in criticism or mockery —that all his works, even the most

beautiful, were just hurriedly tossed off. It is true that Mozart did not like writing.…, He had to be made, even forced, to do it. But once he had been induced to do it and had warmed to the task, it went very quickly. At least in his later years, he could compose with such intense concentration of all his mental powers that he seldom had to make any improvements afterward. Because of this, it could not be said that he wrote as quickly and easily as if it were a trivial occupation; what he wrote had seldom just occurred to him at the time of writing. This was even less the case regarding the general conception and overall structure of the piece in question.

Whether he was alone, or with his wife, or with other people (provided they placed no constraints on him), and particularly during his many journeys by carriage, Mozart had the habit of giving free rein to his imagination to invent new melodies, at the same time occupying his intellect and emotions with arranging, developing, and exploiting the new material. In the process he would often hum or even sing aloud, without realizing what he was doing; he would become burning hot and would brook no disturbance. In this way he completed whole compositions in his head and carried them around with him until he was persuaded to write them down or until he felt the compulsion to get them off his mind. So of course the actual writing process was swift; in fact, while writing the music out, he liked it if people around him were idly chatting, and he would even add the occasional word to the conversation.

On his travels, he came to the home of X., whose twelve-year-old son was showing great promise on the keyboard. Said the boy, "I should like to compose something. How do I start?"

"Don't do anything, anything at all. You must wait."

"But you were composing when you were younger than I am now."

"But I didn't ask! If you have the urge to do it, it compels you and torments you; you *have* to do it, and you do, without asking."

The boy stood abashed and crestfallen as Mozart unleashed this stream of words, and finally said, "I only meant that perhaps you could recommend me a book so that I could learn the proper way to do it."

"Look," Mozart replied more gently, stroking the boy's cheek, "none of that matters. Here, here, and here (pointing to his ears, forehead and heart)—that's where your textbook is. If you have it right in there, then by all means take up your pen, and once you have your composition on paper, you can ask some informed person for an opinion."

Georg Nikolaus Nissen
Biographie W. A. Mozarts, 1828

Mozart's stay in Paris in 1778 was not a success. Baron Grimm, his mentor there, wrote to Leopold to advise against his son's staying any longer.

He is too trusting, too inactive, too easy to catch, too little concerned about the means which could lead to fortune. In order to get on here it is best to be artful, bold, and enterprising; for his own good I wish he had half his talent and twice his acumen, then I would not worry about him....

Letter to Leopold Mozart
from Friedrich Melchior von Grimm
27 July 1778

Irish tenor Michael Kelly (1762–1826), who is credited with creating the parts of Don Basilio and Don Curzio in The Marriage of Figaro, *became a friend of Mozart's in Vienna in the mid-1780s. Here he recalls the playful spirit of the great composer.*

At the period I speak of, the Court of Vienna was, perhaps, the most brilliant in Europe.... All ranks of society were dotingly fond of music, and most of them perfectly understood the science....

I went one evening to a concert of the celebrated Kozeluch's, a great composer for the piano-forte, and...was there introduced to that prodigy of genius—Mozart. He favoured the company by performing fantasias and capriccios on the pianoforte. His feeling, the rapidity of his fingers, the great execution and strength of his left hand, particularly, and the apparent inspiration of his modulations, astounded me. After this splendid performance we sat down to supper, and I had the pleasure to be placed at table between him and his wife, Madame Constanze Weber, a German lady of whom he was passionately fond....

He conversed with me a good deal about Thomas Linley, the first Mrs. Sheridan's brother, with whom he was intimate at Florence, and spoke of him with great affection. He said that Linley was a true genius, and he felt that, had he lived, he would have been one of the greatest ornaments of the musical world. After supper the young branches of our host had a dance, and Mozart joined them. Madame Mozart told me, that great as his genius was, he was an enthusiast in dancing, and noise were made, he instantly left off....

I called on him one evening; he said to me, "I have just finished a little duet for my opera, you shall hear it." He sat down to the piano, and we sang it. I was delighted with it, and the musical world will give me credit for being so, when I mention the duet, sung by Count Almaviva and Susan, "Crudel perchè finora farmi languire così." A more delicious morceau never was penned by man, and it has often been a source of pleasure to me, to have been the first who heard it, and to have sung it with its greatly gifted composer. I remember at the first rehearsal of the full band, Mozart was on the stage with his crimson pelisse and gold-laced cocked hat, giving the time of the music to the orchestra. Figaro's song, "Non più andrai, farfallone amoroso," Bennuci [*sic*] gave, with the greatest animation, and power of voice.

I was standing close to Mozart, who, *sotto voce*, was repeating, "Bravo! Bravo! Bennuci"; and when Bennuci came to the fine passage, "Cherubino, alla vittoria, alla gloria militar,"... the effect was electricity itself, for the whole of the performers on the stage, and those in the orchestra, as if actuated by one feeling of delight, vociferated "Bravo! Bravo! Maestro. Viva, viva, grande Mozart." Those in the orchestra I thought would never have ceased applauding, by beating the bows of their violins against the music desks. The little man acknowledged, by repeated obeisances, his thanks for the distinguished mark of enthusiastic applause bestowed upon him.

Michael Kelly
Reminiscences, 1826

Opera singer Michael Kelly, a friend of Mozart's.

often said that his taste lay in that art, rather than in music.

He was a remarkably small man, very thin and pale, with a profusion of fine fair hair, of which he was rather vain. He gave me a cordial invitation to his house, of which I availed myself, and passed a great part of my time there. He always received me with kindness and hospitality. He was remarkably fond of punch, of which beverage I have seen him take copious draughts.

He was also fond of billiards, and had an excellent billiard table in his house. Many and many a game have I played with him, but always came off second best. He gave Sunday concerts, at which I never was missing. He was kind-hearted, and always ready to oblige, but so very particular, when he played, that, if the slightest

Mozart and Freemasonry

Mozart was twenty-eight when he became a Freemason. During the latter part of his life his fellow Masons proved to be an invaluable source of intellectual, material, and moral support.

Much ink has been spilled over Mozart's links with Freemasonry. It was on 14 December 1784 that he was initiated into the Apprentice degree at the Viennese lodge "Zur Wohltätigkeit" ("Beneficence"), whose grand master was Baron Otto von Gemmingen, whom Mozart had met in Mannheim early in 1778 just before leaving for Paris. The baron, a writer who admired Shakespeare as well as 18th-century French authors Jean-Jacques Rousseau and Denis Diderot, was instrumental in giving Mozart his first introduction to Freemasonry. It was probably due to his intervention and that of Count Karl Heinrich Joseph von Sickingen, the

Title page of the score of the cantata *Die Maurerfreude* (*The Masons' Joy*), 1785.

elector's minister in Paris, that Mozart was introduced in Paris to another composer, also a Mason, François-Joseph Gossec. During Mozart's second stay in Mannheim, at the end of 1778, von Gemmingen is thought to have suggested a project for an opera based on Voltaire's play *Semiramis,* to a libretto written by the baron himself.

The first Masonic lodge was founded in London on 24 June 1717, under the protection of St. John the Baptist, and the movement grew rapidly in Europe and America. Its introduction into Germany was effected by Francis of Lorraine (the future Emperor Francis I, who married Maria Theresa in 1736) after his own initiation in 1731. Despite a papal bull in 1738 condemning it, Freemasonry was tolerated and then openly accepted, and the first Viennese lodge opened in 1742.

In 1780 Maria Theresa was succeeded by her son Joseph II, with whom she had been sharing power since 1765. There was some hostility to the Freemasonry movement, and by 1786 there were only two lodges left in Vienna. Mozart's lodge had by this time merged with others to form one of these, "Zur Neugekrönten Hoffnung" ("New Crowned Hope").

It is not always realized just how perfect a meeting point the Masonic order provided for the intellectual elite in an age that was prey to a host of moral and spiritual doubts and questions to which the church, preoccupied as it was with its political and social role, had no answer. Inspired by traditions derived from medieval corporatism (particularly those of architects and masons, hence the movement's name) and from initiation rites believed to have originated in ancient Egypt, Freemasonry adopted the humanist ideals of the Age of Enlightenment, which transcended religious dogma. These generous ideals were directed toward human happiness, and it is not surprising that the sensitive Mozart was attracted by them.

He had had contact with Masons very early on: In 1767 in Vienna he composed the song "An die Freude" ("To Joy") to a Masonic text as a token of thanks for a doctor who had looked after him during a smallpox epidemic. Several others influenced his life on the path toward initiation: Dr. Franz Anton Mesmer, Tobias Philipp von Gebler (librettist of *Thamos, king of Egypt*), Baron Otto von Gemmingen, Joseph Le Gros (director of the Concerts Spirituels in Paris), Baron Gottfried van Swieten, and the mineralogist Ignaz von Born.

Mozart progressed rapidly to the Fellow degree, granted on 7 January 1785, and then to that of Master, granted shortly afterward. Joseph Haydn was initiated in the same lodge on 11 February, and Leopold Mozart on 6 April. It may well have been Mozart's enthusiasm that persuaded both of them to take this step.

In *Thamos, King of Egypt* (1773), the priests of the sun are a transparently obvious representation of Freemasons benefiting from the Enlightenment; *The Magic Flute* (1791) is often considered a testament to the Masonic movement. The line of progress between the two is direct and logical, confirming that Mozart's involvement with Freemasonry was the result of a progressive process of maturing and not just a sudden and temporary whim.

Michel Parouty

Mozart's Operas

Three operatic traditions were current in Mozart's day: opera buffa (comic), opera seria (tragic, or serious), and the German singspiel, where the dialogue between arias is spoken instead of sung as a recitative. Mozart composed in all three genres, writing seventeen operas in all. The best of these number among the highest pinnacles of musical achievement.

LE NOZZE DI FIGARO
(*The Marriage of Figaro*)

This opera, one of the most popular of all time, is an opera buffa in four acts. Lorenzo da Ponte wrote the text. The first performance took place at the Burgtheater, in Vienna, on 1 May 1786, with Nancy Storace (Susanna), Francesco Benucci (Figaro), Luisa Laschi-Mombelli (Countess), Stefano Mandini (Count), Michael Kelly (Don Basilio and Don Curzio), Francesco Bussani (Don Bartolo), Maria Mandini (Marcellina), and Dorotea Sardi-Bussani (Cherubino). The performance was conducted by Mozart.

Count Almaviva
The Countess, his wife
Susanna, her maid
Figaro, the Count's valet
Cherubino, the Count's page
Marcellina, the Countess' duenna
Don Bartolo, a physician in Seville
Don Basilio, a music master
Don Curzio, a lawyer
Antonio, the chief gardener
Barbarina, his daughter

Act I
In the castle of Aguasfrescas, Figaro and Susanna are about to be married; Figaro is measuring the room which they have been allocated while Susanna tries on her new hat. She is disturbed to find how near the room is to the apartments of the Count, who has his eye on her and may exercise the droit du seigneur. Figaro vows to thwart him.

Susanna (Lucia Vestrio) and Figaro (Giuseppe Naldi) in a London production of *The Marriage of Figaro*, 1817.

Marcellina is scheming with Bartolo; Figaro has been unwise enough to sign a declaration of debt promising to marry her if he cannot pay it off, and she intends to hold him to his promise. Cherubino confides in Susanna that he is thrown into turmoil by any feminine presence, and asks her to intercede on his behalf with the Countess, to prevent him from being banished from the castle for having been too forward with the gardener's daughter.

The Count enters and begins to pay court to Susanna. Cherubino hides behind a large armchair, but the arrival of the music master Basilio forces the Count to hide there too, and Cherubino has only the time to jump into the chair, which Susanna quickly drapes with a dress of the Countess's. The page is soon discovered, and the Count, hearing from Basilio that he has a penchant for the Countess, promptly makes arrangements to get rid of him: He will be made an officer and sent off to battle. Figaro teases him in a famous aria.

Act II

The Countess, alone, sings of her grief that the Count no longer loves her. Figaro enters and suggests a plan to make him jealous: He has had delivered to the Count a note alluding to an assignation made by the Countess. Susanna will feign to accept a secret rendezvous with the Count, but in fact it will be Cherubino in disguise who actually turns up. The two women amuse themselves by planning how to dress Cherubino up as a woman, but while Susanna is offstage looking for a dress, the Count enters. The Countess just has time to bundle the page off into

an adjoining room, which she then locks. The Count, hearing noises, asks questions. The Countess replies that it is Susanna in the next room. The Count decides to force the door and, taking his wife with him, goes to look for tools. Susanna, having returned meanwhile, lets Cherubino out of the anteroom and takes his place. When the Count opens the door, it really is Susanna who emerges, much to everyone's astonishment. Unfortunately, the gardener, Antonio, saw someone leaping from the window. Figaro claims that it was he, not the page. Marcellina chooses this moment to demand her due for the unpaid debt. All this postpones the wedding of Figaro and Susanna.

Act III

Susanna had pretended to accept the Count's rendezvous, but he is suspicious. Meanwhile, in a coup de theatre, Marcellina and Bartolo have discovered that Figaro is their son, kidnapped as a child by brigands. Marcellina drops her previous idea, and another marriage is in view as Bartolo declares his intention of marrying her.

Without saying anything to Figaro, the Countess helps Susanna write a note to the Count arranging the time for the rendezvous. A group of young peasants arrives bringing flowers for the Countess; among them is Cherubino, who is quickly unmasked. Barbarina, the gardener's daughter, springs to his defense. At last Figaro and Susanna's marriage is performed, during which Susanna slips the Count the note. The pin with which it is fastened is to be the sign of acceptance.

Act IV

Night has fallen. Figaro comes upon Barbarina, who is searching for the pin that she has been given to deliver to Susanna from the Count. Furious, Figaro inveighs against the female sex, and posts Basilio, Bartolo, and some servants in the garden to prove his wife's infidelity. Susanna, who has overheard everything, plans to provoke his jealousy further. She and the Countess have exchanged clothes. Cherubino arrives. In the dark, there is a great confusion of mistaken identities. The Count calls his servants, angry at his supposed betrayal by his wife, but the Countess then appears; he is deeply confused and discomfited. She pardons him, and the mad day ends with general rejoicing.

Lorenzo da Ponte (1749–1838), librettist of *The Marriage of Figaro, Don Giovanni,* and *Così Fan Tutte.*

Lorenzo da Ponte tells how the libretto for Figaro *came into being.*

I went to Mozart and...asked him if he would like to compose the music for a play I would write for him.

"I would do so most willingly," he answered at once, "but I'm sure I shan't get it accepted."

"I'll see to that," I replied.

... The greatness of his genius demanded a subject which should be ample, elevated and abounding in character and incident. When we were talking about it one day, he asked me if I could easily adapt Beaumarchais' comedy, *The Marriage of Figaro.* The proposal pleased me very well, and I promised to do as he wished. But there was a great difficulty to be overcome. Only a few days before, the Emperor had forbidden the company at the German theatre to act this same comedy, as it was, he said, too

outspoken for a polite audience. How could one now suggest it to him for an opera? Baron Wetzlar very generously offered to give me a very fair sum for the words and to have the opera produced in London or in France if it could not be done at Vienna. But I declined his offers and proposed that words and music should be written secretly and that we should await a favourable opportunity to show it to the theatrical managers or to the Emperor, which I boldly undertook to do. Martini was the only one to whom I told our great secret, and out of his regard for Mozart he very readily agreed to my postponing writing for him until I had finished *Figaro.*

So I set to work, and as I wrote the words he composed the music for them. In six weeks all was ready. As Mozart's good luck would have it, they were in need of a new work at the theatre. So I seized the opportunity and without saying anything to anybody, I went to the Emperor himself and offered him *Figaro*.

"What!" he said, "Don't you know that Mozart, though excellent at instrumental music, has only written one opera, and that nothing very great?"

"Without Your Majesty's favour," I answered humbly, "I too should have written only one play in Vienna."

"That is true," he replied, "but I've forbidden this *Marriage of Figaro* to the German company."

"Yes," I said, "but as I was writing a play to be set to music and not a comedy, I have had to leave out a good many scenes and shorten a great many more, and I've left out and shortened whatever might offend the refinement and decorum of an entertainment at which Your Majesty presides. And as for the music, as far as I can judge it is extraordinarily fine."

"Very well," he answered, "if that is so, I'll trust your taste as to the music, and your discretion as to the morals. Have the score sent to the copyist."

I hastened at once to Mozart and had not finished telling him the good news when one of the Emperor's lackeys came with a note requesting him to go to the palace at once with the score. He obeyed the royal command and had various pieces performed before the Emperor, who liked them wonderfully well and was, without exaggeration, amazed by them. He had excellent taste in music, as indeed in all the fine arts, and the great success which this piece achieved throughout the world showed clearly that he was not mistaken in his judgement....

A certain Bussani, the stage-manager and costume-keeper, who knew something of every profession except that of a gentleman, hearing that I had introduced a ballet into *Figaro*, ran at once to the Count [Saur, chief of police] and in surprised and disapproving tones said to him, "Your Excellency, the poet has introduced a ballet into his opera." The Count immediately sent for me and angrily began the following dialogue....

"So the Signor poet has introduced a ballet into *Figaro*?"

"Yes, Your Excellency."

"Doesn't the Signor poet know that the Emperor won't have ballets in his theatre?"

"No, Your Excellency."

"Well, Signor poet, I tell you so now."

"Yes, Your Excellency."

"And what is more, I tell you you must take it out, Signor poet."

(This "Signor poet" was repeated in a significant tone as though he meant "Signor ass" or something like it, but my "Excellency" too had its due meaning.)

"No, Your Excellency."

"Have you the libretto with you?"

"Yes, Your Excellency."

"Where is the ballet scene?"

"Here, Your Excellency."

"Well, this is what we do with it." And so saying, he took out two sheets of my play, threw them quietly on the fire and handed me back the libretto, saying, "You see, Signor poet, that I can do everything." Then he honoured me with a second "*Vade*" ["Go"].

I went at once to Mozart who on hearing the bad news was in despair. He wanted to go off to the Count, give Bussani a thrashing, appeal to the Emperor, recall the score—in truth I had a hard task to calm him....

Lorenzo da Ponte
Memoirs, 1828
translated by L. A. Sheppard, 1929

DON GIOVANNI

Don Giovanni is Mozart's masterpiece. With its fundamental ambiguities, this opera, more than any other, provides the richest and most complex account of humanity's metaphysical uncertainties. Through the power of music and the force of genius, the character of Don Giovanni—Don Juan—becomes not only a theatrical hero but a myth. The first performance was held at the National Theater in Prague on 29 October 1787, with Luigi Bassi (Don Giovanni), Felice Ponziani (Leporello), Giuseppe Lolli (the Commendatore and Masetto), Antonio Baglioni (Don Ottavio), Teresa Saporiti (Donna Anna), Catarina Micelli (Donna Elvira), and Teresa Bondini (Zerlina). Mozart was the conductor.

Don Giovanni, a young nobleman
Donna Anna
Don Ottavio, her fiancé
the Commendatore, her father
Donna Elvira
Leporello, Don Giovanni's servant
Zerlina, a peasant girl
Masetto, her fiancé
The setting is a village in Spain.

Act I
In front of the Commendatore's house, Leporello awaits his master, Don Giovanni, grumbling about his conditions of service. Donna Anna, the Commendatore's daughter, comes in indignant pursuit of Don Giovanni, who has attempted to seduce her. Her father challenges Don Giovanni to a duel and is killed. Donna Anna goes to

The graveyard scene in *Don Giovanni*, in a 1789 Mannheim production designed by Joseph Quaglio.

look for help and returns with her betrothed, Don Ottavio. Over her father's corpse she demands vengeance.

Still on the lookout for more women to seduce, Don Giovanni finds himself confronted by Donna Elvira, whom he had abandoned. He makes off, leaving Leporello to recite to the appalled Donna Elvira the catalogue of his master's conquests.

During a village wedding, Don Giovanni leads the bridegroom, Masetto, away and then makes overtures to the bride, Zerlina. Elvira intervenes, and soon afterward Donna Anna and Don Ottavio appear, still searching for the killer of the Commendatore. Don Giovanni (in disguise) volunteers to help them, but Elvira warns them against him. Donna Anna has recognized the assassin's voice and once more calls on Don Ottavio to avenge her father's murder.

Don Giovanni gives a party in his palace. He has invited Zerlina, who has managed to calm Masetto down. Three masked figures present themselves and, invited by Leporello, mingle with the guests. They are Donna Anna, Donna Elvira, and Don Ottavio in search of justice. To Masetto's fury, Don Giovanni has still not given up the idea of seducing Zerlina. Masetto and the three masked characters are not taken in. Zerlina screams and Don Giovanni turns on Leporello, pretending he is the culprit, and manages to get away.

Act II
Still hoping to seduce Zerlina, Don Giovanni has exchanged clothes with Leporello. Elvira appears at her balcony and Don Giovanni serenades her; she yields to his charms, but by the time she has descended from the balcony, he has vanished, leaving her with Leporello. Masetto and his friends come to seek out the seducer. Giovanni, still in disguise, sends them off on a false trail and beats up Masetto, who has to be consoled by Zerlina. Threatened by Ottavio and Anna, Leporello confesses to the subterfuge. Ottavio demands justice, but Elvira hopes Giovanni will come to no harm; despite his infidelities she still loves him. Don Giovanni and Leporello have escaped from their pursuers and find themselves in the graveyard next to the statue of the Commendatore. A spectral voice threatens the libertine, but he defiantly invites the statue to dine with him. Anna has put off her marriage to Don Ottavio. While Don Giovanni is dining, Elvira implores him to mend his ways before it is too late, but he brushes her aside. The statue arrives and invites Don Giovanni to accept a return invitation and shake hands. Giovanni holds out his hand. One last time the statue orders him to repent; Giovanni remains defiant, and the statue drags him down to the depths of hell.

Anna, Elvira, Zerlina, Ottavio, Masetto, and Leporello are left to point out the moral of the story.

The figure of Don Juan fascinated the romantic writers of the 18th century. In the tale of the same name by German writer and composer Ernst Theodor Amadeus (in honor of Mozart) Hoffmann (1776–1822), the narrator goes to the opera, and, stimulated by the music and under the influence of punch, he imagines he meets Donna Anna.

…Zerlina is rescued, and in the powerful, stormy finale [to Act I] Don Giovanni, his rapier drawn, advances to confront his enemies. He strikes Don Ottavio's flimsy stage sword from his hand and forces his way to freedom through the assembled crowd of ordinary folk, throwing them all pell-mell into amusing confusion.

Several times I had thought I sensed, close behind me, a soft warm breathing and heard the rustle of a silk dress: this intimated to me the presence of a woman, but, being deeply absorbed in the poetic world which the opera was opening up before me, I paid no attention. Now, when the curtain fell, I turned to see who it was.... How can I describe my astonishment? Donna Anna, dressed in the same costume that I had just seen her wearing on the stage, was standing behind me, the penetrating gaze of her eloquent eyes fixed on me. I looked at her, speechless; her lips seemed to contract into a slight, ironic smile in which I saw my own foolish face reflected. I felt impelled to speak to her, but, paralysed by amazement or, I might almost say, shock, could not utter a word. At long last, almost involuntarily, these words issued from my mouth: "How is it possible that you are here?" She immediately replied in pure Tuscan that unless I could speak and understand Italian, she would have to do without the pleasure of conversing with me, since she could not speak any other language.

These sweet words fell on my ears like music. As she spoke, her dark blue eyes became even more expressive and every time they flashed I was suffused with a sudden ardour that set my pulse racing and made me tremble in every fibre of my being.

It was Donna Anna, there was no doubt about it. It never occurred to me to wonder how it was possible for her to be on the stage and in my box at the same time. But sometimes a happy dream can blend the strangest elements, and our faith can understand the supernatural and associate it effortlessly with the so-called natural phenomena; similarly in the presence of this strange and magical woman I fell into a state of quasi-somnambulism which enabled me to discover the secret bond which united me with her so closely that she could not have been separated from me even by appearing on the stage.

As she spoke about Don Giovanni and her own role, it was as if the profundity of this masterpiece were being revealed to me for the first time, and I could see clearly into it and discern the fantastical phenomena of an unknown world. She said that music was her whole life, and that often she felt that by singing she could comprehend many things that were locked in the innermost heart and could not be expressed in words. "Yes," she went on, her eyes sparkling and her voice rising, "but all around me remains cold and dead, and when people applaud a difficult roulade or a complicated piece of ornamentation, I feel icy hands clasping my heart!—But you...you understand me: for I know that you too have ventured into the wondrous romantic regions that ring with the heavenly magic of music!"

The interval bell sounded: a sudden pallor drained the colour from Donna Anna's face, which wore no make-up. Her hand went to her heart, as if she felt a sudden pain, and she quietly said, "Unhappy Anna, your most terrible moment is upon you." Then she vanished from the box....

The climax of *Don Giovanni*, when the statue of the Commendatore appears in response to Don Giovanni's invitation to supper—perhaps the most impressive scene in any opera.

I have succeeded in regaining my equilibrium and now I feel capable, my dear Theodor, of putting into words what I believe to be the true significance of this wonderful masterpiece, which I had not grasped until that moment.

If we look at the libretto simply as a story and without attaching any deeper symbolism to it, it is hard to imagine how Mozart could have created such music for it. A *bon vivant*, immoderately fond of wine and women, impulsively invites to supper the stone statue of an elderly father whom he killed in self-defence—really, this idea is not poetically promising, nor, to be frank, does such a man deserve to be singled out by the infernal powers to be made an exhibition of in hell.… Believe me, Theodor! Nature treated Juan as her favourite child, equipped him with everything that brings man close to divinity, raising him above ordinary mortals

and distinguishing him from the cheap products turned out by workshops which are no more than a series of zeros, meaningless unless preceded by a number.

Don Juan was destined to vanquish and to dominate. A strong, handsome body and a mind shaped as living proof that the flame of divinity burned within him; a profound sensibility, a quick intelligence.… But the dreadful consequence of the fall of man was that the devil retains the power to lie in wait for him and to lay snares to catch him, even while he is reaching up towards the infinite heights, thereby proving his divine origins. This conflict between divine and demonic powers constitutes the essence of earthly life, while the final victory represents celestial life. Don Juan was fired by the desire to grasp life as his bodily and spiritual constitution demanded, and the constantly burning desire tingling in his veins drove him to

Elisabeth Schwarzkopf as Donna Elvira and Cesare Siepi as Don Giovanni, in a 1954 Salzburg production conducted by Wilhelm Furtwängler.

seize avidly and continually all the experiences the world could offer, hoping for a satisfaction which always eluded him.... Running from one beautiful woman to the next, enjoying the charms of each with a fervour so intense that it became a destructive intoxication; always believing himself mistaken in his choice, ever hoping to find enduring satisfaction with the ideal woman; it was inevitable that Don Juan would finally admit that life was flat and insipid, and, despising all humanity, turn against the one who, having seemed to be all that was most exalted in life, had caused him the bitterest disillusionment. From then on each act of possessing a woman was not the satisfaction of desire but an irreverent challenge to Nature and its Creator.... His one aspiration is to raise himself above the limitations of this life, but he does so only to be plunged into the depths of hell...

Two o'clock strikes! I feel a thrilling warm breath near me—I sense the subtle odour of fine Italian perfume which was my first intimation of my neighbour yesterday; I am surrounded by a blissful sensation which I feel can only be expressed in music. A stronger current of air moves across the theatre—the strings of the piano in the orchestra vibrate—Heavens! as from a great distance, borne on the wings of a light-toned orchestra in crescendo, I think I hear Anna's voice: "Non mi dir, bell'idol mio!"

Unfold, distant undiscovered land of the spirits!—Djinnistan, faery region where the enraptured soul is filled with ineffable, heavenly anguish and inexpressible joy, and finds itself heaped to overflowing with all that was unattainable on earth!

E. T. A. Hoffmann
Fantasies after the Manner of Callot
1814–5

Composer Charles Gounod (1818–93) revered Mozart, but Paul Dukas (1865–1935), also a composer, has perhaps more penetrating observations to make.

Throughout my life, the score of *Don Giovanni* has been a continual revelation. It has always seemed to me the embodiment of dramatic and musical perfection. In my view it is a peerless, impeccable work; and this judgment is but the humble expression of my gratitude and veneration for the genius to whom I owe the purest, most enduring joys of my life as a musician and composer. There have been a handful of men in history who seem destined to attain, each in his own sphere, a peak higher than which it is not possible to rise: in sculpture, Phidias; in comedy, Molière. Mozart is one of these, and *Don Giovanni* is the peak of his achievement.

Charles Gounod
Mozart's "Don Juan"
1890

One of the particular characteristics of the musical style of *Don Giovanni*, perhaps the most astonishing of all, is the remarkable sobriety of touch with which Mozart obtains effects of extraordinary intensity. From beginning to end, he maintains a concealed current of vibrant expression, allowing it to gather in intensity as the work progresses and finally unleashing it in a torrent when the climax of the action calls for it. Musically speaking, the catastrophe at the end of *Don Giovanni* is the inevitable consequence of the tragic situations that have been building up to it. All the most turbulent and brilliant episodes of the score have lurking within them the hidden threat of the final terrible explosion.

It is interesting to note that Madame de Staël, who held the somewhat unusual opinion that Mozart was ingenious rather than a genius, nevertheless appreciated this duality in the musical expression of *Don Giovanni*. In her book *De l'Allemagne* she writes: "Of all composers it was perhaps Mozart who showed the greatest aptitude and talent for marrying the music to the words. In his operas, especially *Don Giovanni*, he exploits every gradation of drama; the singing is full of gaiety, while the strange, powerful accompaniment seems to reflect the work's somber symbolism." However, she then

modifies this excellent aperçu by adding, "This spiritual alliance between composer and poet does give pleasure of a kind, but it is a pleasure which is born of reflection and, as such, does not belong within the marvel-filled sphere of the arts." This is very like what people were later to say of Wagner.

Paul Dukas
Writings on Music
1948

COSÌ FAN TUTTE

The first performance of Così *was given at the Burgtheater, in Vienna, on 26 January 1790, by Vincenzo Calvesi (Ferrando), Francesco Benucci (Guglielmo), Francesco Bussani (Don Alfonso), Adriana Ferrarese (Fiordiligi), Louise Villeneuve (Dorabella), and Dorotea Sardi-Bussani (Despina). Mozart conducted.*

Fiordiligi, a lady of Ferrara
Dorabella, her sister
Despina, their chambermaid
Ferrando, Dorabella's fiancé
Guglielmo, Fiordiligi's fiancé
Don Alfonso, an old philosopher
The action takes place in Naples.

Act I
In a café, Don Alfonso is discussing with his friends Guglielmo and Ferrando the question of women's fidelity. The two young men are confident of their fiancées, Fiordiligi and Dorabella, but Don Alfonso suggests they should be put to the test. With the help of their servant Despina he announces to the two young ladies that their lovers have to leave immediately for the war. Distraught, they tenderly bid them

adieu. Scarcely have the young men left than Don Alfonso produces two young Albanians, who lose no time in declaring their love, but the two sisters repulse them indignantly—each having failed to recognize that the young man wooing her is her sister's lover in disguise. Ferrando and Guglielmo pretend to take poison in despair; Despina, disguised as a doctor, "revives" them. It is clear that the sisters are not unmoved.

Act II
Encouraged by Despina, the "Albanians" try their luck again. This time Dorabella agrees to exchange the medallion which Ferrando had given her for a pendant offered by the disguised Guglielmo. Fiordiligi resists longer. Ferrando is hurt by his friend's success with Dorabella and becomes convinced of the fickleness of women. More and more distressed, and persuasively urged by Despina and Alfonso to accept Ferrando, Fiordiligi thinks of going to join her fiancé on the battlefield. But, won over by the feigned despair of Ferrando, she gives in to him—to the fury of Guglielmo, observing from a hiding-place.

The two young men resolve to break their engagements, but Don Alfonso convinces them that all women behave in the same way ("Così fan tutte").

At dinner, the two newly formed couples drink a toast to their love. Despina, disguised as a notary, arrives to perform a marriage ceremony, but at that moment trumpets are heard offstage, announcing the return of the armies. The "Albanians" quickly leave; Ferrando and Guglielmo make their entry and appear astonished

to get such a lukewarm reception. All is revealed when Ferrando demands to see his medallion and Guglielmo's pendant is found on Dorabella. Despina removes her mask, and the sisters discover that they have been duped. The couples form up again as at the start, but with no illusions.

English conductor Sir Thomas Beecham (1879–1961) relates the story of his revival of Così Fan Tutte *in London in 1910, and music scholar Charles Rosen discusses the opera's ironic element.*

I then took in hand a short Mozart cycle.... *Così Fan Tutte* proved easily the most interesting; few had ever heard of it, and fewer still seemed acquainted with the music, although it is equal in beauty to anything the composer ever wrote. As one lovely melody followed another until it seemed as if the invention of Mozart was inexhaustible, the whole culminating in the wonderful canon-quartette of the last scene, it was hard to believe that in our age of vaunted culture and education a work like this, then one hundred and twenty years old, was being heard almost for the first time in a great city like London. Admittedly it lacks the breadth and dramatic poignancy of *Don Giovanni*, the brilliant and acute vigour of *Figaro*, or the bright dewy freshness of *Il Seraglio*: nor do we find there any of those solemn intimations which are heard now and then in *Die Zauberflöte. Così Fan Tutte* is a long summer day spent in a cloudless land by a Southern sea.... In *Così Fan Tutte* the dying eighteenth century casts a backward glance over a

Ferrando, disguised as an Albanian, with Fiordiligi (Kiri Te Kanawa), in the 1976 Paris production of *Così Fan Tutte*.

period outstanding in European life for grace and charm and, averting its eyes from the view of a new age suckled in a creed of iconoclasm, sings its swan-song in praise of a civilization that has passed away for ever.

Sir Thomas Beecham
A Mingled Chime: An Autobiography
1944

It should not be concluded that the music becomes more sincere as the characters drop their pretences. Mozart is as direct—and as pretentious —in the one instance as in the other. The irony of the opera depends on its tact; it is a masterpiece of "tone," this most civilized of all aesthetic qualities. There is no way of knowing in what proportions mockery and sympathy are blended in Mozart's music and how seriously he took his puppets.... Even to ask is to miss the point: the art in these matters is to tell one's story without being foolishly taken in by it and yet without a trace of disdain for its apparent simplicity.... Those who think that Mozart wrote profound music for a trivial libretto misunderstand his achievement.... The farewell quintet in the first act is a touchstone of Mozart's success: heartbreaking without ever for a moment approaching tragedy, and delightful without a trace of explicit mockery in the music, it seems to hold laughter and sympathy in a beautiful equilibrium.

Charles Rosen
The Classical Style: Haydn, Mozart, Beethoven
1971

DIE ZAUBERFLÖTE
(*The Magic Flute*)

The Magic Flute was completed in 1791, the year of Mozart's death. The libretto was written by his friend and fellow Mason Emanuel Schikaneder (1751–1812), who also sang the role of Papageno in the first performances. Schikaneder had commissioned a "magic opera" from his friend for the Theater auf der Wieden, of which he was manager. The Magic Flute *was first staged on 30 September 1791, with—in addition to Schikaneder—Franz Xaver Gerl (Sarastro), Benedikt Schak (Tamino), Josepha Weber-Hofer (Queen of the Night), Anna Gottlieb (Pamina), Barbara Gerl (Papagena), and Johann Joseph Nouseul (Monostatos). Mozart conducted the performance.*

Title page of an early vocal score of *The Magic Flute*, showing Papageno and Tamino with the dead serpent.

DIE ZAUBERFLÖTE
eine
GROSSE OPER IN ZWEY AUFZUGEN
fürs
CLAVIER oder PIANOFORTE
von
W. A. MOZART.
Erster Theil

Sarastro, Priest of the Sun
Tamino, a foreign prince
Speaker
the Queen of the Night
Pamina, her daughter
Three Ladies
Three Boys
Papageno, a bird catcher
Papagena
Monostatos, a Moor

Act I

Pursued by a serpent, Prince Tamino is saved by three ladies—not by Papageno, who attempts to take the credit. When Tamino recovers from his faint, the ladies give him a portrait of Pamina, the daughter of their Queen, held prisoner by Sarastro. To punish Papageno for his lies, they padlock his mouth. The Queen of the Night appears and promises Tamino her daughter's hand in marriage if he can rescue her. The ladies remove Papageno's padlock, give him a set of bells, and provide Tamino with a magic flute to protect him.

In Sarastro's palace, Monostatos is pestering Pamina, but Papageno arrives and chases the Moor away. Meanwhile the three boys have conducted Tamino to the portals of the temples of Nature, Reason, and Wisdom. Delighted to know that he will soon meet Pamina, Tamino plays his flute and enchants the wild animals. To escape from the slaves whom Monostatos has sent to catch him, Papageno shakes his bells, and they are enchanted. At this point Sarastro arrives. He comforts Pamina and asks her not to see her mother again. Monostatos appears, followed by Tamino, who has been captured. He and Pamina fall in love at first sight.

Papageno with his birdcage and feather-clad children crown the "Papageno Portal" of the Theater an der Wien, Vienna, by Franz and Anton Jäger. This theater, completed in 1801, took over the role of the Theater auf der Wieden, which had burned down that year. It was the site of many performances of *The Magic Flute* as well as other operas by Mozart.

Act II

Sarastro prays to Isis and Osiris to grant protection to Tamino and Pamina. The first trial that Tamino and Papageno have to undergo is that of silence. They succeed despite the attempts of the three ladies to make them speak. The Queen of the Night gives her daughter a dagger and orders her to kill Sarastro. Monostatos reappears and threatens to denounce Pamina, but Sarastro intervenes. He reassures the young girl again; it is not his intention to seek vengeance on the Queen of the Night. The trials of Tamino and Papageno continue. An old woman appears before Papageno, saying she is his promised bride, Papagena, but disappears again. Tamino, still under the command of silence, is in despair because he cannot speak to Pamina. Papageno finds the old woman again, and she is transformed into a charming girl; but his trials are not yet over and again she disappears.

Pamina, in utter despair, tries to kill herself. She is prevented by three boys, who lead her to Tamino for the final trial, that of fire and water. Papageno, not finding Papagena again, attempts to hang himself, but on the advice of the three boys he shakes his bells again and Papagena reappears.

Monostatos has been persuaded by the Queen of the Night to help him abduct Pamina, but in the face of the Light, the powers of night are vanquished. Pamina and Tamino, finally united, have found the Truth.

The summerhouse where Mozart is believed to have composed *The Magic Flute.*

Alfred Einstein (1880–1952) made the following critical defense of The Magic Flute *in his 1945 biography of Mozart.*

The origin of *Die Zauberflöte*, like that of the Requiem, is covered with a web of legends. Mozart is supposed to have rescued Schikaneder, by means of this work, from financial difficulties; Schikaneder is said to have kept him in good humor during its composition by giving him wine and oysters and to have kept him locked up in a garden-house near the theater....

Mozart is supposed to have hesitated to accept the proposal for fear of a fiasco, for "he had not yet composed a magic opera." All this is nonsense, of course. The work was produced on 30 September and its success grew with every repetition....

The weakness of the libretto—a small weakness, easily overcome—lies only in the diction. It contains a great number of unskilful, childish, vulgar turns of speech. But the critics who therefore decide that the whole libretto is childish and preposterous deceive themselves. At any rate Goethe did not so consider it when he wrote a *"Zauberflöte* Part II," unfortunately unfinished, but full of fairy-tale radiance, poetic fantasy, and profound thought. In the dramaturgic sense Schikaneder's work is masterly. The dialogue could be shortened and improved, but not a stone in the structure of these two acts and of the work as a whole could be removed or replaced, quite apart from the fact that any change would demolish Mozart's carefully thought out and organic succession of keys....

[The plot] seems merely a fantastic entertainment, intended to amuse suburban audiences by means of machines and decorations, a bright and variegated mixture of marvelous events and coarse jests. It is such an entertainment, to a certain extent; but it is much more, or rather it is something quite different, thanks to Mozart. *Die Zauberflöte* is one of those pieces that can enchant a child at the same time that it moves the most worldly of men to tears, and transports the wisest. Each individual and each generation finds something different in it; only to the merely "cultured" or the pure barbarian does it have nothing to say. Its sensational success with its first audiences in Vienna arose from political reasons, based on the subject-matter. Mozart and Schikaneder were Freemasons; Mozart an enthusiastic one, and Schikaneder surely a crafty and active one. The latter used symbols of Freemasonry quite openly in the libretto. The first edition of the libretto contained something rare in such books—two copperplate engravings, one showing Schikaneder-Papageno in his costume of feathers, but the other showing the portal to the "inner rooms," the great pyramid with hieroglyphs, and a series of emblems: five-pointed star, square and trowel, hour-glass and overthrown pillars and plinths. Everyone understood this. After a period of tolerance for the "brothers" under Joseph II, a reaction had set in with Leopold II, and there had begun again secret persecutions and repressions.... Under the cloak of symbolism *Die Zauberflöte* was a work of rebellion, consolation, and hope. Sarastro and his priests represent hope in the victory of light, of humanity, of the brotherhood of man. Mozart took care, by means of rhythm, melody, and orchestral color, to make the significance of the opera, an open secret, still clearer. He began and ended the work in E-flat major, the Masonic key. The slow introduction of the Overture begins with the three chords, symbolizing the candidate knocking three times on the portal; and then in the climactic scene Tamino knocks on three different doors. A thrice-played chord follows Sarastro's opening of the ceremonies in the temple. Woodwinds, the typical instruments of the Viennese lodges, play a prominent part; the timbre of the trombones, heretofore used by Mozart—in *Idomeneo*, in *Don*

Frontispiece of the first edition of the libretto of *The Magic Flute*.

Emanuel Schikaneder.

Giovanni—only for dramatic intensification, now takes on symbolic force.

These Masonic elements had little meaning for the "uninitiated" and have had even less for later generations. What remains is the eternal charm of the naive story, the pleasure in Schikaneder's skill…and the wondering awe at Mozart's music. The work is at once childlike and godlike, filled at the same time with the utmost simplicity and the greatest mastery.

Alfred Einstein,
Mozart: His Character, His Work,
translated by Arthur Mendel
and Nathan Broder,
1946

Musicologist H. C. Robbins Landon, who has made a special study of Mozart and the Freemasons, considers the circumstances surrounding the composition of The Magic Flute, *with its borrowing of the ideals, rituals, and number symbolism of a very secret society.*

It was suggested long ago that the Masons killed Mozart. There are, very simply, two facts which render this theory—which is considered very attractive in some quarters even today—not only unlikely but impossible. The first is that no one killed Schikaneder, who was just as responsible for "betraying Masonic secrets" as Mozart…. And the second reason is equally, if not more, convincing: Mozart's own Lodge held a Lodge of Sorrows for their composer, printed the main speech, and also printed the Masonic cantata (K. 623) Mozart had composed before he died.

The fact of the matter is that Freemasonry in Austria was in acute danger of extinction…[because of] their supposed involvement with the French Revolution…. In the face of such suspicion and hostility, how was Masonry to be protected? How were its greatness and universality to be presented to the general public? The two Masons, Mozart and Schikaneder, decided to write the first Masonic opera—*The Magic Flute.* Wisely, they treated the whole subject in two ways: with dignity, love and respect—as true Brothers—but also not without humour, with even a hint of malicious satire…. The audience in September 1791 went home with the feeling that the Masons were the embodiment of the Enlightenment—and besides, much of the opera was genuine good fun….

Mozart obviously found the amazing diversity of the subject immensely attractive. In the final score, this ranges from the Haydnesque folk-tunes of the music for the "simple" beings, Papageno and Papagena, to the mystical and ritualistic music for Sarastro and his court, and from the mad coloratura of the Queen of the Night...to the inclusion of an antique-sounding north German Lutheran chorale tune, sung by the two men in armour. It was this same diversity that so impressed Beethoven (who in any case disapproved of Da Ponte's texts for the Italian operas as being too frivolous) and which impresses us, too.

H. C. Robbins Landon
1791: Mozart's Last Year
1988

In Idomeneo *and* The Clemency of Titus, *Mozart contravened the conventions of opera seria just as he surpassed those of opera buffa in* The Abduction from the Seraglio. *In all three, Mozart's prime concern was the accurate depiction of human nature.*

IDOMENEO, 1781

Idomeneo, king of Crete, returning home after a prolonged absence, is almost drowned in a storm at sea. He vows to sacrifice to Neptune the first living human being he encounters. Alas, this turns out to be his son Idamante. The latter loves Ilia, the Trojan princess, and is loved by Electra, daughter of Agamemnon. Idomeneo wishes to send his son away to protect him, but a sea-monster comes to threaten the Cretans. The monster, an envoy of Neptune, is killed by Idamante. But Idomeneo must keep his vow. Just before the sacrifice is to take place, a divine voice is heard: Idomeneo is to abdicate in favor of his son, who is to marry Ilia—to Electra's fury. In the general rejoicing, Idomeneo celebrates the return of peace.

DIE ENTFÜHRUNG AUS DEM SERAIL (*The Abduction from the Seraglio*), 1782

Constanze, engaged to Belmonte, has been captured by pirates with her maid, Blonde, and the latter's fiancé, Pedrillo, Belmonte's valet. They have been taken to the palace of Pasha Selim, where they are being detained. With Pedrillo's aid, Belmonte succeeds in tricking Osmin, the keeper of the harem, and freeing the prisoners. But they are caught while fleeing. The Pasha turns out to be a former enemy of Belmonte's father, who had once persecuted him; but he is magnanimous and pardons them all.

LA CLEMENZA DI TITO (*The Clemency of Titus*), 1791

The Roman emperor Vitellius has been deposed by Titus. Vitellius's daughter Vitellia attempts to organize a conspiracy with the help of Sextus, who is in love with her. The young man, who loves and admires the new emperor, hesitates but finally agrees. Learning that Titus has resolved to marry her, having renounced both Berenice and Servilia (Sextus's sister), Vitellia tries to forestall the assassination, but too late. It turns out, however, that Sextus had only attacked one of the conspirators. He is arrested and admits his crime but without compromising Vitellia. Distressed, she confesses to Titus, who, despite his sorrow, grants them all his pardon.

Mozart in the Eyes of Musicians and Critics

The appreciation of Mozart by critics and audiences has varied greatly over the years. He has never failed to excite the interest and admiration of other musicians, however, even when he is out of favor with the general public.

Illustration of a type of viol, from the 18th-century *Encyclopédie* of Denis Diderot and Jean Le Rond d'Alembert.

Two Composers Express Their Views

Nineteenth-century composers Frédéric Chopin (1810–49) and Claude Debussy (1862–1918) reflect on Mozart's talent.

Where the latter [Beethoven] is obscure and seems to lack unity, the cause is not the supposed rather wild originality for which he is esteemed; it is that he turns his back on eternal principles. Mozart never does this. Each voice in Mozart has its own line which, while according perfectly with the other voices, forms its own melody which it follows in the most perfect manner. That is true counterpoint, *punto contrapunto*.

Frédéric Chopin
in Eugène Delacroix, *Journal*, 1823–54

Music must be set free from any sort of scientific approach; its aim must simply be to *give pleasure*. Within these limits it is possible to achieve great beauty. Extreme complication is the antithesis of art. Beauty must be something that can be *felt*, the pleasure it gives must be immediate; it must impose itself on us, or insinuate its way into us, without our having to make the least effort to reach out toward it. Look at Leonardo, look at Mozart. There were two great artists!

Claude Debussy
Monsieur Croche, 1921

A French Philosopher Responds to Mozart's Genius

In one of his best-known works, Hippolyte Taine (1828–93) lauds Mozart's art.

Even when Mozart is joyous he never ceases to be noble; he is never a *bon vivant*, a simple epicurean like Rossini:

He never mocks feelings or slips into vulgar joviality. There is a supreme refinement in his gaiety; when he does indulge in it, he does so gradually, by degrees, because his musical personality is flexible and because in any truly great artist no aspect is missing. But at the heart of him is an unconditional love of civilized, serene beauty.

Hippolyte Taine,
*Life and Opinions
of Thomas Graindorge,* 1867

Shaw Defends Mozart

At the time of the centenary of Mozart's death in 1891, he was not fully appreciated by the public. George Bernard Shaw (1856–1950), who was a music critic in London before becoming a dramatist, was one of his most fervent champions.

Unfortunately, Mozart's music is not everybody's affair when it comes to conducting it. His scores do not play themselves by their own physical weight, as many heavy modern scores do. When a sense of duty occasionally urges Mr. Manns or the Philharmonic to put the G minor or the E flat or the *Jupiter* Symphony in the bill, the band, seeing nothing before them but easy diatonic scales passages and cadences smoothly turned on dominant discords, races through with the general effect of a couple of Brixton schoolgirls playing one of Diabelli's pianoforte duets. The audience fidgets during the *allegro*; yawns desperately through the *andante*; wakes up for a moment at the minuet, finding the trio rather pretty; sustains itself during the *finale* by looking forward to the end; and finishes by…voting me stark mad when I speak of Mozart as the peer of

Bach and Wagner, and, in his highest achievements, the manifest superior of Beethoven.

George Bernard Shaw
"A Mozart Controversy"
The World (a London newspaper)
11 June 1890

A Conductor Considers *The Seraglio*

Sir Thomas Beecham, whose recorded performances of Mozart operas are still prized today, paid tribute to The Abduction from the Seraglio *in his autobiography.*

Here at last we find the full-grown and mature Mozart, emancipated from the traditions and conventions of a style of operatic composition that had held the stage for eighty years and of which his *Idomeneo* is a first-rate example. In *Il Seraglio* we are introduced to a new and living world. Gone from the scene are the pallid heroes and heroines of antiquity, the unconvincing wizards and enchantresses of the Middle Ages and all the other artificial creatures dear to the whole tribe of eighteenth century librettists. In their unlamented place we have ordinary human beings of recognizable mould, singing their joy and sorrows to melody that rings as freshly in our ears today as in those of the Viennese one hundred and sixty years ago.

In songs of the highest excellence the score is exceptionally rich.… But astonishing as is this exhibition of solo virtuosity, it is outrivalled by the ensemble pieces, of which the finale to the second act is the crown. Here we have the first instance on a large scale of that matchless skill with which Mozart could weave together a succession of movements, each representing a different mood or stage in the action, into a complete unity that is entirely satisfying to the musical sense. And as the absolute fitness of the music to the dramatic situation is never in question for a moment, all flows on with a natural ease beyond which human art cannot go. In the last number of all, the Vaudeville, we have a specimen of that haunting strain peculiar to this master, half gay, half sad, like the smile on the face of a departing friend. These tender adieux abound in the later Mozart.

Sir Thomas Beecham
A Mingled Chime

Mozart Becomes the Subject of Detailed Critical Analysis

Two 20th-century critics analyze the composer's craft.

Mozart's way of reaching his listeners is to make use of a faultless technical equipment. His is so smooth and natural a technique as to be very easily overlooked. In fact we are not intended to be made aware of it or to admire it for its own sake: it is merely the means to an end, and in the case of one so supremely gifted a perfectly convenient and untroublesome means, even where it involves appalling difficulties. No parade is ever made of skill or learning. Sometimes, it is true, as in the finale of the *Jupiter* Symphony, sheer pleasure in the exercise of a staggering virtuosity takes hold of Mozart irresistibly; but even there the music remains clear, its surface undisturbed by the polyphonic problems he tackles, so that the hearer who remains unaware of them still enjoys the incomparable flow and polish of the music.

Mozart's sovereign ease in the handling of counterpoint is the very foundation of his style and one of the great differences between him and Beethoven, who happened to find counterpoint difficult—which is not to say that he eschewed it or that, when he faced it, he failed to do justice to his own peculiar genius. What distinguishes Mozart is the fact that he always applied this gift of his, whether he intended to write polyphonically or not, and that, considering how readily contrapuntal writing came to him, he made conscious use of polyphonic skill surprisingly rarely. But it was at the very root of his technique, even where he simply wrote accompanied melody. It is this which explains why his part-writing and his spacing are always, whatever the nature of the musical texture may be at the moment, superbly lucid and limpid.

Eric Blom
in Ralph Hill, *The Symphony*, 1949

In the G minor Symphony [no. 40, K. 550], a work of passion, violence, and grief for those who love Mozart most, Schumann saw nothing but lightness, grace, and charm. It should be said at once that to reduce a work to the expression of sentiments, however powerful, is to trivialize it in any case: the G minor Symphony is not much more profound conceived as a tragic cry from the heart than as a work of exquisite charm. Nevertheless, Schumann's attitude to Mozart ends by destroying his vitality as it canonizes him. It is only through recognizing the violence and the sensuality at the center of Mozart's work that we can make a start towards a comprehension of his structures and an insight into his magnificence.… In all of Mozart's supreme expressions of suffering and

A page from the opening allegro movement of Mozart's Sonata for Harpsichord and Violin in B-flat major, (K. 8), composed in Paris when he was seven. The manuscript, in Leopold's hand, is dated 21 November 1763.

terror—the G minor Symphony, *Don Giovanni*, the G minor Quintet [K. 516], Pamina's aria in *Die Zauberflöte*—there is something shockingly voluptuous. Nor does this detract from its power or effectiveness: the grief and the sensuality strengthen each other, and end by becoming indivisible, indistinguishable one from the other.

Charles Rosen
The Classical Style

A Pianist and Two Sopranos Speak from Their Experience as Performers

Austrian-born Artur Schnabel (1882–1951) was one of the 20th century's outstanding pianists.

I am attracted only to music which I consider to be better than it can be performed. Therefore I feel (rightly or wrongly) that unless a piece of music presents a problem to me, a never-ending problem, it doesn't interest me too much. For instance, Chopin's études are lovely pieces, perfect pieces, but I simply can't spend time on them. I believe I know these pieces; but playing a Mozart sonata, I am not sure that I do know it, inside and out. Therefore I can spend endless time on it. This can probably only be understood by one who has had the same experience. Many colleagues of mine would laugh at me. They would say: "What is the problem? I don't see any problem." Here we come to the absolutely uninvestigatable field of *quality*—the demarcation line between quality and quantity, essence and appearance. Once I was asked by somebody: "How is it that you speak with such reverence and awe of Mozart's profundity?" It was the wife of a star virtuoso to whom I once spoke in almost deliberately exaggerated terms of the depth of Mozart's music, the unfathomable, transcendental qualities. She said: "We too love Mozart, but we think his music is just sweet and lovely and graceful. If your valuation," she continued, "is the right one, Mr. Schnabel, how do you explain the fact that all children play Mozart so well?" I answered: "Well, children have at least one very important element in common with Mozart, namely purity. They are not yet spoiled and prejudiced and personally involved. But these are, of course, not the reasons why their teachers give them Mozart to play. Children are given Mozart because of the small *quantity* of the notes; grown-ups avoid Mozart because of the great *quality* of the notes—which, to be true, is elusive!"

Artur Schnabel
My Life and Music, 1961

German soprano Elisabeth Schwarzkopf (b. 1915), one of the foremost Mozart singers, explains why Mozart presents a uniquely rewarding challenge to vocalists.

Even a naturally frail voice like my own must respond to Mozart's demand for a high degree of vocal deportment and poise. The voice must communicate itself to the audience, but it must also surpass its own standard. Maria Ivogün, my teacher, once said to me, "Be noble, my dear!" At the time I was working on a Mozart concert aria with violin obbligato. The violin has a magical sonority, a radiance in its legato, which the voice must attempt to imitate. In all his operas Mozart wrote marvelous parts for the wind; the singer must listen attentively to each one and reflect in the voice the different tone-colors which Mozart has put into the orchestra. This is why it's so important for a singer to sing Mozart only in the best possible instrumental environment, and with a real "ensemble" of singers. With each different partner you

Elisabeth Schwarzkopf in the role of Donna Elvira in *Don Giovanni*.

find some new aspect or nuance to which you must adapt yourself. It's no use having a lot of vibrato in the voice; it kills Mozart by preventing the voice from blending with the instrumental ensemble. But there is no greater pleasure for a singer than to have to adapt in this way. Mozart makes it a privilege. But it also demands *discipline*!

Elisabeth Schwarzkopf,
interviewed in *Le Point* (a Paris
newsmagazine), 25 October 1982

The much-loved soprano Irmgard Seefried (1919–88) discusses these challenges further.

When I was a student I didn't realize Mozart would become such an important part of my life; only when I got to Vienna did this become apparent. In 1943 I sang Susanna in *Figaro* and the Composer in *Ariadne auf Naxos* [by Richard Strauss] at the State Opera with Karl Böhm—two roles and two composers who have played a large part in my career. Only later did I realize the importance of Mozart for singing Strauss.

Susanna is a long and difficult role; she is on stage almost all the time, and the success or failure of the whole thing depends on her. To sing Susanna you must be a good actress and have a flawless technique. This applies to any Mozart role, of course.

Naturalness

The singer must be able to sing with naturalness and to move naturally about the stage; the voice and body must be in natural harmony with one another. In reality naturalness can only be the result of a great deal of work. There is no shortcut to singing Mozart well. There is no such thing as a Mozartian voice, or a born Mozart singer; you become one after much effort and sacrifice. The Mozart singer is therefore an actor able and willing to undertake endless variations in this combination of voice and body. This is absolutely fundamental, especially for the recitatives, which are so difficult to master—a kind of sung speech or spoken song. It is the recitatives that contain much of the dramatic characterization. There must not be any abrupt break between recitative and aria—it all follows on and you must

Title page of a 19th-century vocal score of *The Marriage of Figaro*.

pass from the one to the other, whether legatissimo or staccato, with complete naturalness—I use that word again. The line can be straight or curved, but it must never be broken. I learned a lot on this point from the Italians. When we were at La Scala with [conductor Herbert von] Karajan it was no joke: The cast was made up of Italians and Germans or Austrians, a difficult and potentially explosive mixture. There was great rivalry. Karajan said, "I warn you, this will be a flop." La Scala had its own particular way of singing Mozart. But in the end all went well. The Italians taught me a lot about recitatives, that staccato way of singing *parlando* which is so hard for those born north of the Alps.

The Importance of Ensemble
To sing Mozart you have to enjoy collaboration. We had a team of singers and orchestral players and used to rehearse together every day. Nowadays this sort of practicing no longer happens: Singers are usually jetting around and their roles are rehearsed by understudies! And the young ones want to become stars and sing Mozart only en passant…. But that's unwise of them. This teamwork was the strength of Vienna. The conductors, including [Karl] Böhm and [Josef] Krips, formed a strong, homogeneous unit with the singers. They worked, thought, and rehearsed together, and the result was a uniquely harmonious blend. Performances under Böhm and Krips were pure, clear, and perfect. They would not tolerate the slightest sloppiness or approximation— everything always had to be perfect. That's why we had to train so intensively. Italian voices are trained

Irmgard Seefried as Susanna in *The Marriage of Figaro.*

toward producing a big sound, but this is catastrophic for Mozart. Someone once asked a great Italian tenor what he thought of a performance of [Strauss's] *Der Rosenkavalier.* He replied, "Poco voce, poco voce!" (too little voice). Mozart's view of the human voice was quite un-Italian; he disliked any bawling or vocal slovenliness. Mozart must be sung with grace, poise, and restraint, with humility and simplicity. It needs discipline like at the Spanish Riding School.

Singing in ensemble does not mean giving up your own personality. It means adding your personality to the total effect. In Mozart, the voices are quite interchangeable: The key to it is to find the right colors and intonation to suit each partner. Passage work is vitally important. The chest voice is dangerous: Too much vocal weight is enemy number one, for the voice must remain flexible, malleable, and light. Up and down, up and down, *ad libitum.* If you have a big voice, you can sing Wagner more or less well, but for Mozart volume is irrelevant—you have to have complete control and be able to sing pianissimo when necessary, and that means you have to practice technique every day—scales, passage work, breathing, *vocalize*.

A schooling in Mozart is a hard one, but it's the best of all. Armed with this sophisticated technique, which is a different conception of singing, you can tackle any other composer, including modern ones, provided they lie within your vocal range. I'm thinking particularly of the composers of the second Viennese School. An understanding of beautiful *singing* as distinct from a beautiful *sound* is what matters for Mozart—in fact, a succession of beautiful sounds is a guarantee of deadly boredom. To sum up: Mozart is lightness with depth, both tangible and impalpable.

I am a Mozart singer because I have always loved singing Mozart, a composer with whom I have had a privileged relationship. Pamina is probably my favorite role, but I have had immense, intense pleasure from my other roles too. I remember a *Don Giovanni* at Salzburg that was quite unforgettable, with Ljuba Welitsch as a magnificent Donna Anna and [Elisabeth] Schwarzkopf superb as Elvira. But the whole team—[Anton] Dermota, [Erich] Kunz, etc.—was wonderful. Each conductor conducted differently; each had a different vision —Böhm, Krips, Karajan. Furtwängler adored Mozart, although it wasn't quite his scene. He had to work hard at it. I remember some very beautiful things conducted by him. Krips enjoyed the musical quality of the ensemble and produced some grandiose finales. Böhm was the one for precision and purity.

All of us worked in the service of

Mozart, and after much toil, trial, and tribulation we found the immense joy of encountering true genius in him. There were no individual stars. The ensemble itself was the star.

Irmgard Seefried, interviewed in *L'Avant-Scène Opéra* (a French opera magazine), October 1985

Instrumental Performers Give Valuable Insight into Performing Mozart on the Piano and Violin

Musicologists and pianists Eva and Paul Badura-Skoda compare the pianos of Mozart's time to those of today.

If any musician is now interested in gaining a clear idea of the sound of instruments in Mozart's time, he should examine the changes that have taken place in this direction during the past two hundred years. The tonal picture has altered in many respects; the developments of recent centuries have aimed at a greater volume of tone, greater compass, better intonation and, very often, greater ease of performance....

In achieving greater volume, the character of piano tone has been steadily altered. It seems that the human ear only reacts favourably to very bright sounds, rich in overtones, when they are not very loud. Forte [loud], these sounds tend to make a sharp, shrill effect, and fortissimo [very loud] they are almost unbearably strident. So it is not at all surprising that, in comparison with Mozart's piano, even Beethoven's, and *a fortiori* the pianos of the nineteenth and twentieth centuries, have not only a fuller, louder tone, but also one that is darker and usually duller. This was an inevitable development of the manufacture of pianos. Compared with the modern piano, Mozart's piano, with its many overtones, produces an extraordinarily thin, translucent effect, sharply defined and "silvery." The instrument was more delicately built, the strings were thinner, and this made its tone relatively weak....

It should not be supposed that our piano is capable of subtler nuances; the Mozart pianos of [Andreas] Stein and [Anton] Walter, for instance, were clear and very bright in the upper register, and this made it easier to play cantabile and with full colour. The lower notes had a peculiar round fullness, but none of the dull, stodgy sound of the low notes of a modern piano. Whereas the tone becomes steadily thinner toward the top, the highest register sounding almost as if pizzicato, the full sound of the bass is by far the most satisfying register of the Mozart piano. The strings are so thin that chords in the bass can be played with perfect clarity even when they are closely spaced. On a modern piano such chords usually sound sodden and earthy.

It is certainly true that nowadays we are accustomed to a much greater degree of noise than in earlier times—street noises, the thunder of railways

Mozart's piano. Built in Vienna by Anton Walter in 1780, it was bought in 1784 by Mozart, who had it fitted with a special sustaining device.

and the roaring of aeroplanes, the stentorian tones of larger-than-life loudspeakers in cinemas and at public gatherings, and enormous orchestras in the concert hall. If we were to re-create the absolute intensity levels of the eighteenth century, it is certain that the resulting sound would at first seem much too thin and lacking in penetration. We must reconcile ourselves to the fact that a forte, if it is to sound like one to us, must in acoustical terms be louder than in Mozart's time. For all that, even today a Mozart forte should still not have the volume of tone of a Wagner forte... since for Mozart, *forte* may already mean "full out," whereas in Wagner *f* [forte] is only rarely a dynamic climax, in view of his use of dynamics as loud as *fff* [fortississimo].

Eva and Paul Badura-Skoda
Interpreting Mozart on the Keyboard
1962

Thoughts on technique from Dutch violinist Jaap Schröder (b. 1925).

Clearly it is the bow which brings the music to life; when the bow ignores the "breathing" quality of the music as the result of constant pressure, players look for a different way to enliven the performance. During the nineteenth century this task fell to the newly invented *portamento*; our century has adopted the constant vibrato. But both these devices stand in the way of musical clarity: *portamento* covers up the openings in the articulation, while vibrato (when used as a device of tension) destroys the transparent quality of the sound. And a lack of clarity is damaging to the scores of Mozart....

One aspect of Mozart interpretation that has been much influenced by the increasing inherent tension of post-classical instruments is the tempo. Playing the classical violin, with its gut strings and with the older, more flexible bow, helps to rediscover a sense of speed that is closely related to the human pulse and does not need extreme values at both ends of the scale.... Speed must always serve the purpose of the musical discourse if it is not to degenerate into empty brilliance. No more than the spoken word, and for the same reasons, should music be hurried.

For modern musicians, going back to the older instruments of the classical period constitutes first of all a process of un-learning, of abandoning a technique that is based on a high degree of tension. Even if a sense of frustration is experienced in the beginning (our tradition of a muscular approach is useless and damaging to the instrument and to the music), this first reaction is most often followed by a refreshing sense of freedom. Relaxation leads to elasticity; constant pressure is replaced by a multitude of differentiated impulses. And once these important principles have taken root in our way of interpreting the classical repertoire, it is certainly possible to achieve a workable compromise with modern instruments. In calligraphy the old quill pen is the ideal tool, but once we have mastered this art of beautiful writing and know how to differentiate the individual strokes, we will be able to produce artistic results even with a fountain pen.

Jaap Schröder,
"A Performer's Thoughts on
Mozart's Violin Style,"
Perspectives on Mozart Performance,
edited by Larry Todd and
Peter Williams, 1991

Mozart in Literature

Mozart has been the subject of numerous works of literature —from the comic to the tragic, from verse drama to prose narrative. The following extract is from Mozart and Salieri, *a play by the great Russian writer Aleksandr Sergeyevich Pushkin (1799–1837).*

A masked figure from the film version of *Don Giovanni.*

In this story, Pushkin makes use of the idea—which originated with Mozart himself—that the composer was poisoned by his inferior rival Antonio Salieri in a fit of jealousy. Mozart is depicted as infuriatingly carefree and casual.

Scene 1 (*A room in Salieri's house*)

SALIERI: Justice, they say, does not exist on earth.
But justice won't be found in heaven either:
That's plain as any simple scale to me.
Born with a love of art, when as a child
I heard the lofty organ sound, I listened,
I listened and the sweet tears freely flowed.
Early in life I turned from vain amusements;
All studies that did not accord with music
I loathed, despised, rejected out of hand;
I gave myself to music. Hard as were
The earliest steps, and dull the earliest path,
I rose above reverses. Craftsmanship
I took to be a pedestal of art:
I made myself a craftsman, gave my fingers
Obedient, arid virtuosity....
I envy—I profoundly envy. Heaven!
O where is justice when the sacred gift,
Immortal genius, comes not in reward
For toil, devotion, prayer, self-sacrifice—
But shines instead inside a madcap's skull,
An idle hooligan's? O Mozart, Mozart!

(*Enter Mozart.*)
MOZART: You've seen me!—Damn! I have a joke for you—I wanted to surprise you.

SALIERI: You here ...

MOZART: Yes, I came to show you
something: on my way
I passed an inn, and there I heard a
fiddle...
A funnier sound you never heard,
Salieri—
A blind old tavern fiddler's "Voi che
sapete!"
Priceless! I couldn't help myself; I've
brought him
To entertain you with his art. Come in!

(Enter a blind old man with a violin.)
Something by Mozart, please. *(The old
man plays an aria from* Don Giovanni.
Mozart roars with laughter.)

SALIERI: How can you laugh?

MOZART: How can you *not* laugh? Oh
Salieri!

SALIERI: No: I'm not amused when
some appalling dauber
Tries his Raphael Madonna out on me,
I'm not amused when wretched
mountebanks
Dishonour Dante with their parodies.
Be off, old man.

MOZART: Wait—drink my health with
this.

(Exit old man.)
You're out of sorts today, Salieri. Well,
I'll come another time.

SALIERI: What have you brought?

MOZART: Oh, nothing much. The other
night insomnia
Plagued me again, some thoughts went
through my head.
I wrote them down. I wanted your
opinion...

You haven't time for me.

SALIERI: Oh Mozart! I—
No time for you? Sit down; I'm
listening.

MOZART: *(At the piano)* Now,
Imagine...whom?—Myself, a little
younger;
And I'm in love—not deeply, just a bit;
I'm with a pretty girl, or friend—say
you,
I'm happy... Then: a vision of the
grave,
Or sudden darkness, something of the
kind.
Listen. *(Plays.)*

SALIERI: You came to me with this, and
stopped
To listen to a tavern scraper! Mozart,
You are unworthy of yourself.

MOZART: You like it?

SALIERI: What grace! What
depth—what bold magnificence!
Mozart, you are a god: you do not
know it,
But I know, I know.

MOZART: Nonsense! Well...who
knows?
I'm starving though, in my divinity.

SALIERI: Let's dine together, come—the
Golden Lion.

MOZART: Gladly. But first I'll have to
tell my wife
I won't be home for supper.

Alexander Pushkin
*Mozart and Salieri:
The Little Tragedies*, 1830
translated by Antony Wood, 1982

Mozart in Theater and Film

By the 19th century, Mozart had already become a subject for the stage. It was inevitable that in the 20th he would appear on the screen. However, the mixture of fact and fiction remains highly problematic.

In his play *Amadeus* (first produced in London in 1979), Peter Shaffer—like Pushkin—explored the notion of the "undeserved" nature of Mozart's genius.

In the play, Salieri nourishes a sense of injustice because the divine gift of music has been withheld from him and bestowed upon the carefree, worthless Amadeus—"beloved of God." Shaffer combines this with the picture, drawn in Wolfgang Hildesheimer's 1977 biography, of Mozart's peculiar, childlike psychology and Constanze's low character.

The portrait was based to some extent on real documents, but it was distorted for theatrical effect, and one may regret that it has gained such wide currency—chiefly through director Milos Forman's internationally successful film version (1984).

In Milos Forman's film version of Peter Shaffer's *Amadeus,* Mozart was played by Tom Hulce, and Constanze by Elizabeth Berridge (left, a scene from their wedding). F. Murray Abraham appeared as Salieri (top).

Several of Mozart's operas have also become the subject of films. Swedish director Ingmar Bergman's *The Magic Flute* (1974) is a wonder-filled pantomime, part comic and part serious. Some scenes take place in an 18th-century theater near Stockholm, while others are invented entirely by Bergman's visual imagination.

With his *Don Giovanni* in 1979, director Joseph Losey initiated a wave of enormously popular film versions of operas, and Italian baritone/actor Ruggiero Raimondi became a household name.

Below: For the overture of *Don Giovanni,* Losey invented a fantastic sequence set in a Venetian glassworks, where Don Giovanni (Raimondi, wearing white in the center) and the other characters stare into the furnace as into the flames of hell.

Above: Pamina (Irma Urrila) and Tamino (Josef Kostlinger) undergo the trial by fire in Bergman's *The Magic Flute.*

Chronology

	Mozart	The Arts	Historical Events
1756	Born in Salzburg (January 27)	Publication of Leopold Mozart's *Violin Method*	Beginning of the Seven Years' War
1761	First composition		
1762	Travels with Leopold and Nannerl to Munich; family travels to Vienna	Premiere of Christoph Willibald Gluck's *Orfeo and Euridice*	
1763	Family leaves Salzburg for three years; first sonatas for violin and piano		End of the Seven Years' War
1764	Arrives in London; meets Johann Christian Bach		
1765	Travels to the Netherlands		Joseph II becomes Holy Roman emperor
1766	Visits Paris and other European cities; returns to Salzburg	Jean-Honoré Fragonard paints *The Swing*	Mason-Dixon Line drawn
1767	Performances of *Die Schuldigkeit des Ersten Gebots* and *Apollo and Hyacinthus* in Salzburg; first piano concertos; family travels to Vienna	Premiere of Gluck's *Alceste*; death of Georg Philipp Telemann	
1768	Writes *La Finta Semplice* and *Bastien and Bastienne*; returns to Salzburg		
1769	Wolfgang and Leopold travel to Italy		Birth of Napoleon Bonaparte
1770	Meets Padre Martini; named knight of the Golden Spur by the pope; *Mitridate, Rè di Ponto*; inducted into the Bologna Accademia Filarmonica; premiere of *Mitridate* in Milan	Birth of Ludwig van Beethoven; Handel's *Messiah* performed in New York	Daines Barrington gives a lecture on Mozart to the Royal Society in London; Louis XVI of France marries Marie Antoinette, daughter of Empress Maria Theresa
1771	Return to Salzburg; travels to Italy with Leopold; *Ascanio in Alba* performed in Milan; return to Salzburg		
1772	Hieronymus Colloredo becomes archbishop of Salzburg; *Lucio Silla*; travels to Milan for premiere		
1773	Performance of *Exsultate, Jubilate* in Milan; Piano Concerto no. 5	Goethe writes first version of *Faust*	Boston Tea Party
1774	Symphony no. 29; piano sonatas; begins *La Finta Giardiniera*	Premiere of Gluck's *Iphigenia in Aulis*	

1775	Premiere of *La Finta Giardiniera* in Munich; violin concertos		Beginning of American Revolution
1776	*Haffner* Serenade	Birth of E. T. A. Hoffmann	Declaration of Independence
1777	Travels with Anna Maria		Death of Elector Maximilian III
1778	Falls in love with Aloysia Weber; Symphony no. 31 (*Paris*); Anna Maria dies (July)	Ludwig van Beethoven presented by his father as six-year-old prodigy	
1780	Meets Emanuel Schikaneder	First modern piano built in Paris	Death of Empress Maria Theresa
1781	*Idomeneo* premieres in Munich; breaks with Archbishop Colloredo; moves to Vienna		
1782	*The Abduction from the Seraglio*; Symphony no. 35 (*Haffner*); marries Constanze Weber	Death of Johann Christian Bach	
1783	Birth and death of first child (Raimund Leopold); C minor Mass; visits Salzburg		Great Britain recognizes independence of the United States
1784	Piano concertos; String Quartet in B-flat; birth of second child (Karl Thomas); becomes a Freemason	The play *The Marriage of Figaro* presented in Paris	
1785	Begins *The Marriage of Figaro*		
1786	Premiere of *Figaro* in Vienna; birth and death of third child (Johann Thomas)		Death of Frederick the Great of Prussia; succeeded by Frederick William II
1787	Death of Leopold Mozart; *Eine Kleine Nachtmusik*; birth of fourth child (Theresia)	Luigi Boccherini made court composer in Berlin	
1788	Premiere of *Don Giovanni* in Vienna; death of daughter Theresia		Austria declares war on Turkey
1789	Visits Prague, Dresden, Leipzig, and Berlin with Prince Lichnowsky; birth and death of fifth child (Anna Maria); begins *Così Fan Tutte*	William Blake publishes *Songs of Innocence*	First United States Congress meets in New York; beginning of the French Revolution
1790	Premiere of *Così* in Vienna		
1791	Birth of sixth child (Franz Xaver Wolfgang); writes *La Clemenza di Tito*; premiere of *The Magic Flute* in Vienna; begins the *Requiem*; dies (December 5)		Coronation of Leopold II as German emperor; ratification of the Bill of Rights in the United States

Further Reading

Anderson, Emily, ed., *Letters of Mozart and His Family,* Norton, New York, 1986

Badura-Skoda, Eva, and Paul Badura-Skoda, *Interpreting Mozart on the Keyboard,* trans. Leo Black, Da Capo, New York, 1985

Beecham, Sir Thomas, *A Mingled Chime: An Autobiography,* Da Capo, New York, 1976

Blom, Eric, *Mozart,* Littlefield, Lanham, Maryland, 1978

Branscombe, Peter, *W. A. Mozart: Die Zauberflöte,* Cambridge University Press, New York, 1991

Da Ponte, Lorenzo, *Memoirs of Lorenzo da Ponte,* Da Capo, New York, 1985

Dent, Edward J., *Mozart's Operas: A Critical Study,* AMS Press, New York, 1955

Deutsch, Otto Erich, *Mozart: A Documentary Biography,* Stanford University Press, California, 1966

Einstein, Alfred, *Mozart: His Character, His Work,* Oxford University Press, New York, 1965

Girdlestone, Cuthbert M., *Mozart and His Piano Concertos,* Dover, New York, 1952

Hildesheimer, Wolfgang, *Mozart,* trans. Marion Faber, Farrar, Straus and Giroux, New York, 1982

Hill, Ralph, *The Symphony,* Scholarly Press Inc., St. Clair Shores, Michigan, 1961

Holmes, Edward, *The Life of Mozart,* Greenwood, Westport, Connecticut, 1980

Landon, Howard C. Robbins, *Mozart and the Masons,* Thames and Hudson, London, 1991

———, *Mozart and Vienna,* Schirmer, New York, 1991

———, *Mozart: The Golden Years,* Schirmer, New York, 1989

———, *1791: Mozart's Last Year,* Macmillan, New York, 1988

Landon, Howard C. Robbins, ed., *The Mozart Compendium,* Schirmer, New York, 1990

Mann, William, *The Operas of Mozart,* Oxford University Press, New York, 1982

Mersmann, Hans, *Letters of Wolfgang Amadeus Mozart,* trans. M. M. Bozman, Dover, New York, 1972

Novello, Vincent and Mary, *A Mozart Pilgrimage: Being the Travel Diaries of Vincent and Mary Novello in the Year 1829,* transcribed and completed by Nerina Medici di Marignano, ed. Rosemary Hughes, Da Capo, New York, 1982

Pushkin, Aleksandr, *Mozart and Salieri: The Little Tragedies,* trans. Antony Wood, Dufour Editions, Chester Springs, Pennsylvania, 1987

Rosen, Charles, *The Classical Style: Haydn, Mozart, Beethoven,* Norton, New York, 1972

Sadie, Stanley, *The New Grove Mozart,* Norton, New York, 1985

Schnabel, Artur, *My Life and Music,* Dover, New York, 1988

Shaw, George Bernard, *The Bodley Head Bernard Shaw,* Dan H. Lawrence, ed.,The Bodley Head, London, 1981

Todd, Larry, and Peter Williams, eds., *Perspectives on Mozart Performance,* Cambridge University Press, New York, 1991

In Other Languages

Bauer, Wilhelm A., and Otto E. Deutsch, eds., *Mozart: Briefe und Aufzeichnungen,* 1962

Buenzod, Emmanuel, *Mozart,* 1930

Dukas, Paul, *Ecrits sur la Musique,* 1949

von Grimm, Baron Friedrich Melchior, *Correspondance Littéraire, Philosophique et Critique,* 1877–82

Nissen, Georg Nikolaus, *Biographie W. A. Mozarts,* ed. Constanze (Mozart) Nissen, repr. 1964

Reiniger, Lotte, *Mozart, die Grossen Opern, mit Scherenschnitten,* 1987

Discography

Operas

The Abduction from the Seraglio (K. 384) Rothenberger, Popp, Gedda, Unger, Frick, Vienna Philharmonic Orchestra/Krips (EMI); humor and tenderness in the great Viennese tradition. Also try the historic Beecham recordings (EMI)

Così Fan Tutte (K. 588) Schwarzkopf, Otto, Merriman, Simoneau, Panerai, Bruscantini, Philharmonia/ Karajan (EMI). Captures the Italian verve of the opera and the charm of the young Schwarzkopf

Don Giovanni (K. 527) Schwarzkopf, Sutherland, Sciutti, Waechter, Taddei, Alva, Cappuccilli, Frick, Philharmonia Orchestra/Giulini (EMI)

Idomeneo (K. 366) Hollweg, Schmidt, Palmer, Yakar, Equiluz, Zurich Opera House Mozart Orchestra/Harnon-court (Teldec). Opera seria transfigured by lively direction

The Magic Flute (K. 620) Dermota, Seefried, Kunz, Lipp, Loose, Weber, Vienna State Opera Chorus, Vienna Philharmonic Orchestra/Karajan (EMI); a miracle of poetry. Salminen, Blochwitz, Hampson, Gruberova, Bonney, Scharinger, Zurich Opera Chorus and Orchestra/ Harnoncourt (Teldec)

The Marriage of Figaro (K. 492) Della Casa, Gueden, Danco, Poell, Siepi, Dickie, Corena, Vienna Philharmonic Orchestra/Kleiber (Decca); an inspired conductor and wonderful teamwork in the cast. Seefried, Jurinac, Hongen London, Kunz, Vienna Philharmonic Orchestra/Karajan (Angel)

Religious Works

Mass in C Minor (K. 42) Hendricks, Perry, Schreier, Luxon, Vienna Singverein, Berlin Philharmonic Orchestra/Karajan (Phillips)

Requiem (K. 626) Mathis, Hamari, Ochman, Ridderbusch, Vienna State Opera Choir, Vienna Philharmonic Orchestra/Böhm (Deutsche Grammophon)

Symphonies

Complete Symphonies Academy of Ancient Music/ Schröder, Hogwood (Oiseau-Lyre); for those seeking performance on period instruments. Other classic recordings include those by Klemperer, Walter, Böhm, Jochum, and Szell

Works for Piano

Complete Piano Concertos Barenboim, English Chamber Orchestra (EMI). Perahia, English Chamber Orchestra (CBS). Two great artists at their peak

Complete Piano Sonatas Barenboim (EMI)

Individual Sonatas Pires, Uchida, Haskil, Badura-Skoda, Arrau, Brendel, Fischer

Works for Strings

Complete String Quartets Amadeus Quartet (Deutsche Grammophon)

Complete String Quintets Budapest Quartet, Trampler (CBS)

Complete Violin Concertos Perlman, Vienna Philharmonic Orchestra/Levine (Deutsche Grammophon). Suk, Prague Chamber Orchestra/Hlaváček (Supraphon/ Eurodisc)

Violin Sonatas nos. 20, 24, 25–8, 30, 32, and 33 Perlman, Barenboim (Deutsche Grammophon). Perfect coexistence

Works for Wind and Brass Instruments

Clarinet Concerto K. 622 Pay, Academy of Ancient Music/ Hogwood (Oiseau-Lyre). Leister, Berlin Philharmonic Orchestra/Karajan (EMI). The Berlin magic

Clarinet Quintet (K. 581) Hacker, Salomon Quartet (Amon Ra/Saydisc). A fine interpretation on period instruments

Flute Concerto (K. 313) and Concerto for Flute and Harp (K. 299) Rampal, Vienna Symphony Orchestra/ Guschlbauer (Erato), with Laskine and Paillard Ensemble (for *Concerto for Flute and Harp*) (Erato)

"Haffner" Serenade (K. 250) Dresden Staatskapelle/ Harnoncourt (Teldec)

Horn Concertos Brain, Philharmonia/ Karajan (EMI). A historic recording, still the most poetic

Serenade for 13 Wind Instruments (K. 361) Vienna Mozart Wind Ensemble/ Harnoncourt (Teldec). A vital new interpretation

List of Illustrations

Index

Photograph Credits

Archiv für Kunst und Geschichte, Berlin 12, 13, 14–5a, 24, 26a, 27a, 32a, 36a, 37al, 37ar, 46b, 50, 51, 58, 66, 68–9a, 91a, 95, 96–7, 98, 100, 107, 108–9b, 110b, 112, 120–1, 122–3, 124–5, 152, 173. Artephot/Bibliothèque Nationale, Paris 94b. Artephot/Mandel, Paris 162. Artephot/Nimatallah, Paris 20–3. Artephot/O'Hana, Paris 53a, 53b. Artephot/Percheron 54–5. Harry R. Beard Collection, Theatre Museum, London 147. Bibliothèque Nationale, Paris 74b, 126–7a, 171. Bildarchiv der Österreichischen Nationalbibliothek, Vienna 101b, 138, 166. British Film Institute Stills, Posters and Designs, London 181a. Cahiers du Cinéma, Paris 178. Charmet, Paris 24–5. Dagli-Orti, Paris 18, 26b, 31, 36–7, 49, 67, 73a, 92–3, 102–3, 104–5, 116–7, 118b, 119a, 121r, 123r. Edimedia, Paris 72–3a. Enguerand, Paris 157. E. T. Archive, London 15, 48, 60, 61, 91b, 93. Explorer Archives, Paris 30b, 94a, 110a. Fayer, Vienna 174. Giraudon, Paris 27b, 33, 100–1, 115a. Giraudon/Lauros, Paris 70. Greater London Photograph Library 143. Heliopolis Verlag, Tübingen 1–9, 116l, 117ar. Emily Lane 163. Magnum/Erich Lessing, Paris 14l, 16, 17, 38, 52, 68–9b, 80–1, 99, 106, 113, 114, 119b, back cover. Mozarteum, Salzburg 17, 19, 35, 133, 176. Municipal Museum, Salzburg 64, 105, 131. Musée Carnavalet, Paris 78–9. National Gallery, London 140, front cover. Réunion des Musées Nationaux, Paris 28–9, 39, 44–5, 63, 76, 77. Roger-Viollet, Paris 30a, 34, 40–1, 54a, 126–7b, 133, 136–7, 146, 155, 157. Royal College of Music, London 130. Scala, Florence 11, 32–3, 42, 43b, 56–7, 85, 90. Theatermuseum, Munich 154. Top/J. P. Charbonnier, Paris 158. Victoria and Albert Museum, London (photograph Eileen Tweedy) 150

Text Credits

Acknowledgment is gratefully made for use of material from Eva and Paul Badura-Skoda, *Interpreting Mozart on the Keyboard,* Barrie and Rockliff, London, 1962 (pp. 175–7); Sir Thomas Beecham, *A Mingled Chime: An Autobiography,* Hutchinson, London, 1944, reproduced with the permission of Shirley, Lady Beecham (pp. 160–1, 169–70); Eric Blom's chapter on Mozart in Ralph Hill, *The Symphony,* Harmondsworth, 1949, reproduced by permission of Penguin Books, Ltd (p. 170); Alfred Einstein, *Mozart: His Character, His Work,* trans. Arthur Mendel and Nathan Broder, Cassell and Co., London, 1946 (pp. 164–6); H. C. Robbins Landon, *1791: Mozart's Last Year,* Thames and Hudson, London, and Macmillan, New York, 1988 (pp. 166–7); Aleksandr Pushkin, *Mozart and Salieri: The Little Tragedies,* trans. Antony Wood, 1982, 2nd revised edition, Angel Books, London, and Dufour Editions, Chester Springs, Pennsylvania, 1987 (pp. 178–9); Charles Rosen, *The Classical Style: Haydn, Mozart, Beethoven,* Copyright © 1971 by Charles Rosen, used by permission of Faber and Faber, London, and of Viking Penguin, a division of Penguin Books USA Inc. (pp. 161, 170–1); Jaap Schröder's essay in Larry Todd and Peter Williams, eds., *Perspectives on Mozart Performance,* Cambridge University Press, 1991 (p. 177); George Bernard Shaw, *Shaw's Music,* Dan H. Lawrence, ed., in *The Bodley Head Bernard Shaw,* The Bodley Head, London, 1981, by permission of the Society of Authors on behalf of the Bernard Shaw Estate (p. 169)

Michel Parouty, born in 1945, has an arts degree
and further qualifications in philosophy and musicology
from the universities of Poitiers and Bordeaux, in France.
After spending some time as a teacher, he turned to
journalism in 1979, joining the staff of the magazine *Opera
International.* He is now joint chief editor of the French
classical music publication *Diapason,* and has been a
contributor to many other international publications on
the arts. In 1986 he coauthored a guide to symphonic
music, and he has just published an edition of
La Traviata in France.

Translated from the French by Celia Skrine

Project Manager: Sharon AvRutick
Typographic Designer: Elissa Ichiyasu
Assistant Editor: Jennifer Stockman
Design Assistant: Penelope Hardy

Library of Congress Catalog Card Number: 93–70490

ISBN 0–8109–2846–9

Copyright © 1988 Gallimard

English translation copyright © 1993 Harry N. Abrams, Inc., New York,
and Thames and Hudson Ltd., London

Published in 1993 by Harry N. Abrams, Incorporated, New York
A Times Mirror Company

Printed and bound in Italy by Editoriale Libraria, Trieste

DISCOVERIES™

Wolfgang Amadeus Mozart lived only a brief
thirty-five years, during which he knew both great joy
and great grief—and composed wondrous music that
was to enrich the lives of millions. He wrote his first
minuet at the age of six; later years were to bring a
profusion of symphonies, chamber music, and operas.
His story has become a legend. Mozart has often been
presented as a simpleminded boy with a miraculous
musical gift, but the truth is both more complicated
and more exciting.

$12.95

9 780810 928466

51295

ISBN 0–8109–2846–9